I WILL
FIND
YOU

I WILL
FIND
YOU

SOLVING KILLER CASES *from*
MY LIFE FIGHTING CRIME

DETECTIVE LT. JOE KENDA

CENTER
STREET®

NEW YORK   NASHVILLE

Center Street
Hachette Book Group
1290 Avenue of the Americas, New York, NY 10104
centerstreet.com
twitter.com/centerstreet

First published in hardcover in 2017.
First Trade Paperback edition: September 2018.

Center Street is a division of Hachette Book Group, Inc. The Center Street
name and logo are trademarks of Hachette Book Group, Inc.

The publisher is not responsible for websites (or their content)
that are not owned by the publisher.

The Hachette Speakers Bureau provides a wide range of authors for speaking events.
To find out more, go to www.HachetteSpeakersBureau.com or call (866) 376-6591.

Cover and title page image courtesy of Investigation Discovery

Print book interior design by Timothy Shaner, NightandDayDesign.biz

Library of Congress Cataloging-in-Publication Data has been applied for.

ISBNs: 978-1-4789-2241-4 (trade paperback), 978-1-4789-2240-7 (ebook)

Printed in the United States of America

LSC-C

10 9 8 7 6 5 4 3 2 1

For Kathy, Dan, and Kris

CONTENTS

Picture a murder case as a spinning top on a table. It is made to spin. It spins perfectly. You as a detective should admire it for as long as necessary to determine the parameters of the case. If you touch it too quickly or too firmly in the wrong place, it scoots off the table and disappears—and you never get it back. You only have one chance to get it right. You can make it unsolvable if you don't know what you are doing on that first touch.
—Retired Police Detective Joe Kenda

Hugging wasn't big in my family, growing up. We were more like the Addams Family than the Waltons. Vacation trips were rare, so it was a major deal when my parents decided to take my brother and me to the Pittsburgh Zoo.

Our first stop at the zoo was the Primate House. As we approached I spotted this sign. It said: "Around this corner, you will see the most dangerous animal on earth."

Intrigued, I ran around the corner and there stood a mirror, a big floor-to-ceiling mirror reflecting the image of all the people walking around the zoo, including me. I stood and looked at that mirror for a long, long time as I thought about the sign's message.

The concept of humans as dangerous beasts really struck me. It was a moment of epiphany. I wondered if it were true. *Could we be the most dangerous creatures on the planet?*

I pondered that question so long, my mother yelled at me to keep moving along with the rest of them. The thought of humans as murderous predators lingered in my mind.

Throughout my twenty-three and a half years in law enforcement, I confirmed that it was indeed true, time and again. I saw firsthand that while most other animals kill only for need, humans can and will kill for pleasure and other sordid reasons.

I became a homicide detective because I wanted to investigate why humans kill each other—and because I wanted to solve the worst of the worst crimes. They throw you in jail for life or execute you for murder, so, I reasoned, murder must be the worst offense, and I wanted to put away the worst of our species. I did put a lot of them away; not enough, but a lot.

If you want to know what it is like to investigate homicide, come with me and I'll show you. Be warned, however. You may not want to see the realities of murders committed by the most dangerous killers in our world. If you have an interest in the truth, you are reading the right book. If you don't think you can handle the darkest aspects of human nature, then you might want to put this book down, because it will get real in a hurry.

As you may or may not know, I was a police officer for the city of Colorado Springs, Colorado. For nineteen years of my career there, I was a homicide detective. I was involved in 387 homicide investigations. I solved 92 percent of them. So, you can say I did a good job 92 percent of the time, or you could say I was the idiot who couldn't figure out 8 percent of his cases.

Those unsolved cases still haunt me, but I loved my job, and I want to make it clear that I was never the Lone Ranger out there solving cases on my own. Please understand this book offers my personal reflections and recollections, I was always working with teams of law enforcement professionals, including my supervisors, fellow detectives, and patrol officers who contributed their guidance and skills in all of these cases. I never would have solved any of them without their support and assistance.

As with every law enforcement agency, ours had many individuals with unique talents. We had one guy who could open any lock, another who could plant (court-approved) cameras, phone taps, and monitors, and others who were like ghosts when tailing and surveilling suspects. If I needed information stored on a computer we'd seized, I called our in-house tech genius who was like Sherlock Holmes with a keyboard. Whenever we had a tough undercover job that required both brains and brawn, we had a man for that too. They were all major contributors to our investigations.

Over the years, I also benefitted from the experience of my co-workers. My bosses yelled at me and called me an idiot quite often, early in my career, and they were right. You learn from people who know what they are doing and your skills increase thanks to their guidance. That is how you grow as a professional.

I served under five different police chiefs during my career. Each had his own leadership style, but they were all wonderful professionals whom I learned from. All of those I worked with deserve credit for the successful investigations mentioned in this book, not just yours truly.

I loved working with them in solving crimes and taking criminals off the street. I would have done it for free, though my wife might have objected. I saw it as a mission. If a monster does horrible things to another person, you can stand up or you can remain seated. I stood up for the victims of murder. I was proud of that.

As much as I enjoyed catching nature's worst killers, the darkest aspects took a toll on me and my family. I turned in my resignation on the day that I lost control of my emotions and came dangerously close to becoming like those I'd hunted.

After recovering my sanity, I knew it was time to retire before someone had to come after me. I thought I could close the door on my memories and wall them off. I thought that, in time, I could put the horrors I'd seen behind me.

I was wrong, so wrong.

Fortunately, I found another way to reclaim my life and my sanity. Or, I should say, a way found me.

We recently began filming our seventh season of *Homicide Hunter* for the Investigation Discovery network. Initially we did six shows per season. Now we are filming twenty. We've hit almost 30 million viewers in the United States, and the show is seen in 178 territories around the world. They tell me that's all very good in the broadcasting business.

What matters most is that telling my stories is cathartic. It's a way of releasing the grief and the horror accumulated over my career as a homicide detective and police officer. I have written this book for the same reason; sharing these stories eases the burden of carrying them. It also puts my experiences in law enforcement into perspective. I've come to see them as simply a part of my past, and, thankfully, not nearly as important and influential in my life as the love of my wife, my son, and my daughter.

Going public with these stories has had another unexpected effect. People seem to connect in a more positive way with me now. When I worked as a policeman, I didn't feel a lot of love or respect. I used the animosity on the streets to drive myself, to do a better job. The killers, their families, and those who feared me made no bones about it. They despised me.

My life was threatened innumerable times. They also threatened to kill my wife, my kids, and my dog. I felt hatred.

The striking part is now that I'm on television, the reverse has happened. I actually feel appreciated. Strangers want to talk to me in airports and malls and on the golf course during my backswing.

I am not the most adept person at social media, but there are at least six *Homicide Hunter* fan pages on Facebook, including one called: "Kendamaniacs."

That page recently featured a "Where's Waldo" poster and the message: "Lt. Joe Kenda is the reason Waldo is hiding."

What, me? A folk hero?

Could it be a sign of the impending apocalypse that there is a Detective Joe Kenda line of souvenir coffee cups, T-shirts, tote bags, and smartphone cases? Or my own lineup of wines, including a My, My, My Merlot?

After twenty-three years dwelling on the dark side of humanity, I am enjoying the light, and I enjoy sharing my stories. I don't know why this is true, or where the storytelling gene came from. There certainly were no other storytellers among my surly and contentious family as I was growing up.

Most of them were too busy trying to kill each other, or threatening to kill each other. So, being a homicide detective felt like home to me.

PART I

EARNING MY STRIPES, MY LUMPS, AND MY NIGHTMARES

ONE

SHIT MAGNET

The Colorado Springs Police Department was still an old-school force when I joined it in 1973. Most of the officers were military veterans with at least ten years on the job. College degrees were rare. Brawn, quick fists, and street smarts were the primary traits needed for advancement.

Rookies didn't get weeks of classroom training before hitting the streets like they do now. Instead they paired you with a veteran partner who showed you the ropes. They had the new guys ride with partners for just two or three weeks until we got to know procedures and the city. Most patrol officers cruised solo, but we didn't get our own patrol cars until we earned them by proving we could survive on the street. There wasn't a written test for that. Usually it meant getting bloody.

I earned my patrol car about two weeks into the job. We were dispatched to the White Spot, a twenty-four-hour drive-in and eat-in restaurant on the city's West Side where trouble was always likely. The typical crowd was drunk and disorderly. After midnight, it was all downhill from there.

My training partner and I were dispatched around 1 a.m. on a call from a cook who said, "A cop is getting killed in here." That got our attention. Upon arrival, yours truly ran inside the joint only to find this mountain of a guy slowly strangling one of our officers on the lunch counter. The cop's face was turning blue.

I waded in with my adrenaline pumping from a volatile mix of fear and anger. I grabbed a fistful of the bad guy's greasy hair and slammed his face onto the lunch counter with my full weight behind it. In my fury, I had not observed a stainless-steel cream dispenser on the countertop. I did not intentionally flatten the dispenser with his face, but that was the result.

Facial bones and cartilage were crushed. Blood spurted everywhere. I thought I had killed him. Everyone else thought the same.

I backed off. The restaurant went dead silent. My partner called for an ambulance. I checked the cop who'd been taking a beating. He was battered and gasping for air, but he'd be okay.

His assailant would need facial reconstruction. When he looked in the mirror and saw the scars, he would not remember me fondly.

Had I gone too far? I wondered if I'd just ended my career before it officially began. I shouldn't have worried. The captain of patrol thought it was really cool that a rookie had so boldly rushed in to assist another officer. The fact that I had smashed in the bad guy's face was worth extra bonus points.

The next day, without fanfare, I was awarded my own patrol car. My reputation as a head-banging street cop was made. The White Spot incident grew into an urban legend of sorts. That was helpful, but it also tagged me with a reputation for attracting trouble. That pattern continued for my entire twenty-three years and six months on the job.

Even as a rookie, I was always getting shot at or attacked by drunks. None of the other cops wanted to be around me. "You're a shit magnet," they'd say, and they were right. Take for instance my first fight call at Fred's Bar, another West Side dive.

Fred's, which is now blessedly out of business, served the

cheapest beer to the lowest of lowlifes. The dump dated back to World War II. They hadn't wiped down the bar since V-J Day. The charming clientele was known for sucking down beer and pissing it out without ever leaving the bar. I'm serious. The regulars didn't mind the filthy decor or the reeking odor because they contributed to it.

I was dispatched to Fred's one night on a fight call. Standard operating procedure would have been to wait for backup, a cover officer, but chairs and tables were flying and the situation was already out of hand. So, I went in as the Lone Ranger. And who did I find inside the bar kicking everyone's ass? A linebacker-sized Native American wearing red patent leather shoes and tossing people around like rag dolls.

He was a beast.

"You are under arrest!" I announced.

The beast responded not as I'd hoped.

One giant hand grabbed my crotch. The other wrapped around my neck. He then hurled me like a sack of potatoes through the front picture window of the bar with such force that I flew over the sidewalk and bounced off the side of my own patrol car parked on the street.

I was still lying in the gutter, checking for broken parts, when my backup arrived. He surveyed the scene, chuckled, and inquired, "Do you think you need some help here?"

"Yeah, I think so," I mumbled.

We didn't have Tasers back then, unfortunately. Instead, we entered Fred's with nightsticks drawn. By my estimate, we swung and connected with our mighty nemesis at least fifty times.

We didn't hurt him. He just got tired and gave up.

A few months later, I met his more-evil twin. The radio dispatcher said there was a fight in the men's room of the bus station. I'd grown smarter. This time I waited for reinforcements.

Again we encountered a Native American of impressive stature, probably six feet five inches and 280 pounds. When we entered, he was calmly coiffing his dark locks in the mirror. At his feet were three guys bleeding and unconscious.

He didn't acknowledge our presence until we drew our nightsticks.

Then he looked up and said, "Does your mother know you boys are out?"

That comment was my first hint that we were in for the fight of our lives. By the time we locked the cuffs on him, my uniform shirt was in shreds and I'd lost about three handfuls of hair. We brought him down, but we paid for it.

After a while, my shit magnet reputation spread beyond the police department and into the community at large. One night a neighbor, who also belonged to our Catholic parish, came knocking. I opened the door and he handed me a package.

"Everybody in the church got together and bought you this," he said.

It was a bulletproof vest, one of the first developed for police work. My neighbors and fellow parishioners were very kind. They didn't want me to die on the job. I wore that vest even though it was heavy and uncomfortable. I didn't want to disappoint my benefactors.

WILD WEST SIDE

My assigned patrol area, the West Side, was a hot zone. You won't find it on the travel brochures showing Pike's Peak, the Garden of the Gods, or Red Rock Canyon. It was not the new and shiny part of Colorado Springs. While there is a great deal of natural beauty within its boundaries, the city had its fair share of crime and violence.

In those days, especially, Colorado Springs retained some of its Wild West heritage, thanks to a diverse and particularly well-armed population that included residents of an army base, two air force bases, the U.S. Air Force Academy, the Cheyenne Mountain nuclear bunker, the U.S. Olympic Training Center, and more conservative evangelical churches than you could ever count.

My first patrol area, the West Side, had more bars than churches. Sleek Olympians and shiny military brass were not among the patrons. Most West Siders were born there and they would die there, often prematurely. There were good, hardworking people in the neighborhood, but I never got to meet them unless they'd become victims of a crime. Otherwise, I only met the dirtbags, the crazies, and the drunk and disorderly.

I'd been a cop for all of ten days when I was dispatched on a domestic disturbance call at 2 a.m. These are always volatile situations. You never know what you are rolling up on when drinking, drugs, and weapons are in play. This seemed like a low-grade squabble at first, though the presence of a Great Dane wandering around the front yard did catch my attention.

The complainant wife announced from the front porch that she wanted her husband arrested. I asked if she had a particular reason, preferably one punishable by law.

"We are getting a divorce. That's my dog. He wants it, but it's my dog. He won't let me take it."

When she saw that I wasn't impressed by that scenario, she tossed out another mitigating factor: "He has a gun."

I called for backup.

Hubby then joined us on the porch. He did not have a gun, but he and the ex-to-be resumed their vitriolic debate over the not so Great Dane, who appeared to be embarrassed by its warring owners.

I was already feeling sorry for the dog when my backup came around the corner with lights flashing. My sympathies intensified when the Great Dane dashed out into the path of the oncoming patrol car.

The big dog was dead on impact.

"I'm so sorry 'bout your dog, ma'am," my fellow officer said as he stepped out of his squad car.

The dead Dane made their marital dispute a moot point. The couple fell silent.

Such was life on the West Side. Most residents abandoned hope before it abandoned them. This was fitting because that section of Colorado Springs, the original center of an old Gold Rush boomtown, had a history of abandonment.

The original section of town was called Colorado City. It was a shithole, but so were most Old West towns. Still, its glory days lasted less than a week.

Historians will tell you that Colorado City was named the territorial capital on November 5, 1861, at a meeting of the legislature in Denver. When the legislators actually ventured into the crappy little town for their first official session, they looked around and decided they'd made a mistake.

They were so appalled, they packed up and left. Five days later, the legislators named Denver the state capital.

DYING FOR A FIGHT

By the time I arrived, Colorado Springs had swallowed up the original site of Colorado City, which became the woeful West Side neighborhood. You may think I'm exaggerating the neighborhood's lowly quality of life, but how many knock-down, drag-out brawls have you been to in a funeral home?

It was a Saturday morning. I was on patrol around 10 a.m. and I thought my morning would be peaceful at least until the local lizards crawled out of their hangovers. I thought wrong.

I was dispatched to join the other West Side patrol officer who had responded to a "disturbance" call at the local mortuary. I pulled up behind his squad car. He was standing outside the funeral home. There was nothing going there.

We walked up to the main doors, opened them, and gazed upon a mourning crowd like no other. About twenty men and women in their funeral finery were engaged in a riotous, rolling fistfight, going at it like packs of rabid dogs. Sport coat sleeves were ripped off. Ties were flying sideways. Purse strings were being deployed as garrotes for choking.

After exchanging WTF glances, my fellow officer directed my gaze to the center ring, where there stood an open casket with not one, but two occupants. The undead one was kneeling on the corpse of the not-so-dearly departed, hammering punches into his pasty face. *Bam! Bam! Bam!*

Maybe the assailant thought, no blood, no foul? Whatever the case, there would be no resting in peace for this deceased dude. I couldn't help but bust a gut laughing for a second, then we rushed in to save the dead from further abuse. By the time we cuffed his aggrieved attacker, the dead guy's jaw was shattered and one eye was drooping from its socket. The carefully applied funeral home makeup was smeared all over the fists of the postmortem mugger.

We made the executive decision to go with a closed-coffin ceremony from that point. Our backup arrived and cops streamed into the funeral home doors. We subdued all of the other grieving friends and family members trying to kill each other. One of them had a skull fracture thanks to being hit with a metal folding chair.

During our follow-up interrogations, we learned that early in the service, several mourners had shouted out epithets cursing the deceased as a no-good son of a bitch. Hell was suggested as his final destination and, as a result, hell was unleashed. Even the most decorated veterans among my coworker cops said they'd never seen anything like that. Privately, the brawling mourners reminded me of my own family of battling Bohunks back in Pennsylvania.

THE BALKAN WARS IN COAL COUNTRY

My boyhood home was in Herminie, Pennsylvania, a little coal town outside of Pittsburgh where many of my family members worked and sometimes died in the deep shafts underground. The Ocean Coal Company owned the two local coal mines, creatively naming them Herminie No. 1 and Herminie No. 2.

The entrance to each shaft was surrounded by company housing, cheaply built brick duplexes. If you took a job with Ocean Coal, you were awarded one side of a duplex. Your rent came directly out of your paycheck, as did the grocery bills from the company-owned store. They owned your soul.

Herminie's Main Street was lined with bars, thirteen of them in a town of two thousand coal-stained souls. When workers surfaced blinking and coated in coal dust each day, they headed first to the bars. Eventually they stumbled home to wash up and sleep it off. Most miners were immigrants who had few other options for employment.

My grandparents came from their native Slovenia to the United States in 1913 to escape the turmoil that led to World War I. They were among the few Kendas to make it out. The Nazis killed most of them in World War II. In my grandfather's native village, Čezsoča, on the Soča River, there is a war memorial, an obelisk built to commemorate members of the local resistance who were assassinated by the Germans. The Germans lined them up and machine-gunned them. There are seven men named Kenda on that obelisk.

My paternal grandfather was among the many Slovenian immigrants drawn to the Pittsburgh area by coal jobs. I never knew my grandfather Josef. He was killed in a mine cave-in in 1933. He was an experienced miner and, the story goes, he was working one day when he sensed that a collapse was coming. He could have saved himself, but he ran to his sons—my father and my uncle—and shoved them out of the shaft. Then the walls collapsed on my grandfather. He was killed saving his boys.

Whenever the story of his death was told to me as a child, it was always emphasized that my grandfather was so acutely aware of conditions in the mine that he alone felt the collapse coming. As a young fan of Sherlock Holmes, I was already aware of the importance of being observant of your surroundings. This frequently told family story sealed that in my mind. It probably helped me become a better detective because I trained myself early on to make note of everything around me, just like the grandfather I was named after.

I suppose you could say that was something positive to take away from such a tragic family event. My father, on the other hand, took his usual dark and negative approach. He actually blamed his brother, also named Joe, for my grandfather's death. He said his brother was lazy and their dad always felt he had to stay on him. My father decided that my grandfather was in that dangerous section of the mine on the day he died because he had to motivate my "lazy" uncle.

As a result, my dad and his brother never spoke to each other after my grandfather was killed. Uncle Joe was not even permitted in our house. When I grew old enough to realize I had an uncle in town whom I'd never met, I began visiting him. He welcomed me, but said my father wouldn't let him come around us.

My father was tough, stubborn, persistently sullen, and unforgiving. My mother was Irish, born Virginia Morrissey, which you'd think would give her at least a sense of humor, but she took on the Bohunk mentality after marrying my father. It leaked into her within minutes. She became just as unforgiving and vindictive as him.

My mother was especially mean to the two women who dared to marry her sons and steal them away from her. For my wife, Kathy, the shunning began as soon as we started dating. You see, Kathy was not my mother's choice. I chose her, and that pissed off Mom for the rest of her life.

It didn't help that I met my future wife while on a blind date arranged by my mother and her best friend. I was a sophomore at Greensburg Central Catholic High School when my mom pressured me to take her friend's daughter to a basketball game, even though I didn't like her, or basketball.

The friend's daughter was a nice enough redheaded girl, another Bohunk offspring like me. I had no reason to truly dislike her, other than the fact my mother had matched us up. My mind and my eyes wandered during our date. I was sitting in the stands at the game with her when I looked up and spotted the prettiest young lady I'd ever seen in my life.

I remember the moment like it was yesterday. She had blond hair and blue eyes and she was wearing a camel-hair skirt and camel-colored vest and a white blouse. I thought, *Wow, who is that?* And before I knew it, I'd left my date on the bench and walked up the stands.

Then I started talking to the love of my life, Mary Kathleen Mohler. We're still talking, most days. We dated all through high school and then married after Kathy graduated from Duquesne University with a nursing degree on December 26, 1967. My mother never got over it.

She held a grudge until the day she croaked—forty years after our wedding. As we were leaving Mom's funeral, I looked at my wife and said, "You are in luck: Your mother-in-law no longer hates you, because she is dead."

DIPLOMATIC DESIGNS

I had to negotiate my way around so many volatile and warring personalities growing up that my first career choice was international
diplomacy. It seemed like a logical move at the time. I majored in
political science as an undergrad at the University of Pittsburgh.
Then I attended Ohio State University, thinking I'd get a master's
degree in international studies. I had romantic notions of being the
suave chargé d'affaires at the U.S. embassy in Paris, but the State
Department had other ideas when I applied. They told me it was
more likely that I'd end up pushing paper somewhere in the wilds
of Africa. Worse, they said I couldn't take Kathy because it was too
dangerous.

I was already souring on the thought of working for the foreign
service when I attended a State Department briefing for potential
employees. The briefing was led by a noxious CIA guy whose worldview was considerably darker than mine at the time. I had served in
the Air Force Reserve while in college and I had a patriot's view of
my country. I thought the United States was the benevolent guardian of liberty around the world.

The CIA man made my country sound more like a manipulative and exploitive bully. All he could talk about was overthrow-
ing governments, protecting our sources of oil, and assassinating
anyone who stood in the way of our need to dominate the globe.
His vision of America was not the same as mine. I'm a right-or-
wrong, black-and-white kind of guy. I wanted no part of his preda-
tory worldview.

I returned to campus feeling dejected, with just a few hours of
grad school needed to complete the degree that I no longer really
wanted. The final blow came one day in a big classroom while we
were waiting for our professor to show up. I looked at the guy sitting next to me and for the first time, I realized that he seemed a lot
older than me. So, I asked him his age.

"I'm thirty-nine," he said.

I was shocked.

"You're still in school? Have you ever had a job?"

"No," he said. "I go to school full-time."

I closed my notebook, stood up, and walked out. I was married with our first baby at home. It was time for me to leave academia behind and get a real job. The problem was I didn't have a plan B when I left Ohio State. So, I made the mistake of my life. I joined my father in his business. I know what you are thinking: *They don't teach common sense in college.*

My father was not a joy to be around, but he was a fairly successful, street-smart guy. Dad spoke several languages and he tracked spies in the United States as an army intelligence officer during the war. He didn't work in the mines, like most of the adult males in our town. He was severely injured in a train wreck while tracking a suspected spy aboard the train. His neck and back were broken and one leg was badly mangled. He spent several years recovering in military hospitals.

Initially the doctors thought he'd never walk again. He proved them wrong out of pure spite. He had to wear a corrective shoe paid for by the government, which gave him an odd gait. Still, he was able to get around and he regained most of his physical strength eventually.

Since his disability ruled out mine work, my dad got a loan from his parents and bought the local wholesale newspaper distributorship. The Herminie News Company handled deliveries of the *Pittsburgh Press* and *Pittsburgh Gazette* and our local county paper, the *Tribune Review.* It was a labor-intensive business with long hours.

Dad had two trucks. One of them delivered papers to newsstands and drop-off points for paper boys. The other delivered to rural subscribers. I worked for him on the truck from the age of eight, while also holding down a huge paper route. At fourteen I took over the rural motor route even though I wasn't of legal age to drive.

When Dad asked me to join his company, I thought the plan was to help him expand and then, one day, I'd take it over so he could retire. Dad had his own plan based on the indentured servitude model. I was the indentured servant. He didn't think of me as the new owner in training. He thought of me as "the help."

My old man put me to work twenty-nine hours a day, eight days a week and he paid me squat. Worse, I had two shifts, splitting my day between early morning and evening deliveries. It seemed like I was either working or exhausted from working, which didn't allow much time for my wife and the kids. They came one right after the other. Our son, Daniel, was born in February 1970 and our daughter, Kristin, followed in October 1971.

Kathy had little help from me with the kids in those early days because I worked so much, a pattern that would continue through most of our marriage. Her frustration in those early days was salted with embarrassment because she had to borrow grocery money from her parents due to my lowly wages. My wife put up with this situation for about two years before she staged a vodka and orange juice protest strike. It wasn't pretty, she freely admits that, and I'll let her fill you in.

I am very good at stretching a dollar, but it got to be embarrassing because we couldn't make it to the end of the month without borrowing from my parents. Joe was either working or asleep, or if he was awake he didn't want to deal with the kids and me so he'd go out with his friends. This wasn't working for me, or us. One night, I put the kids to bed while he was still out with his buddies. While I waited for him to get home, I made myself a vodka and orange juice. Then I made another one. By the time he got home, I was absolutely shitfaced.

When he walked in the door, I said we need to talk.

His expression was "Oh shit."

I told him what I thought of him working for his parents and what they were paying him, and I probably tossed in a few other things. Basically, I said this wasn't working and he needed to find another job or I was out of there with the kids.

The next morning, I woke up with a monumental headache. Joe was staring at me.

"Do you remember anything about last night?" he asked.

I said, "Do you want a synopsis or chapter and verse?"

Once again his expression said, "Oh shit."

Joe had been talking for a long time about maybe becoming a cop. He thought it would suit him, based on stories he'd heard from his favorite uncle, his mother's brother who was a Colorado State Patrol officer. He had also talked about one day moving to Colorado Springs, where he'd visited his mother's parents as a boy. I gave him a year to apply there and some other places. I didn't care if he got a job within a year, I just wanted him to make the effort. Something had to change. We weren't making it.

FLIGHT OF THE KENDAS

Kathy was serious, no doubt about it. I agreed with her that being employed by my father wasn't working out for us, financially or any other way. We needed to put my parents in the rearview mirror, where they deserved to be. My wife and I talked many nights about places we might like to live and Colorado Springs was on the list. We'd visited my mother's brother and other family there. We loved the mountains and the clean air. We especially loved how far it was from Pennsylvania.

A Colorado move was still a dream when, just a few weeks after our first discussion, a pilot friend asked if I wanted to take a quick trip to Colorado Springs with him aboard his boss's $3 million jet. I'd managed to get my pilot's license in my very little free time, so this was an invitation I couldn't pass up.

The pilot had to drop the boss's son off at the Air Force Academy, which I figured would give me time to put in an application at the Colorado Springs Police Department. We flew there on the designated day. I borrowed a car from the local airport's fixed base operator and drove to the city of Colorado Springs personnel office. There I met the personnel director, Norman Gieseker, a friendly guy who delayed his lunch plans to talk to me for a few minutes.

He was impressed that I was a college graduate applying for a police officer's job, because they didn't have many in the department back then. It also might have helped when I told him I was only in town for a couple of hours because I'd flown from Pennsylvania in a private jet to deliver a kid to the Air Force Academy.

Norman let me take the police exam application test right there at his desk, sitting in his nice leather chair, while he went to lunch. He even promised he'd review my test when he got back. Colorado Springs was looking like a nice city to work for.

The test seemed easy enough. I left it on Norman's desk and returned to the airport. We flew home and over the next few weeks while I waited to hear from Colorado Springs, I also applied for police jobs in Pittsburgh and nearby Greensburg, figuring it couldn't hurt.

It always takes a long time for a police department to check out applicants, so it was a couple of months before I heard from anyone. As luck would have it, the first call came from Norman, the personnel director for Colorado Springs. He offered me a job as a city patrol officer and I took it without hesitation.

Norman said I should report for work on March 6, 1973.

I promised him I'd be there.

Then I went to tell my wife we were moving to Colorado and far from my family, so she had no call to divorce me—yet.

Later, I'd give her plenty of reasons to kick me to the curb.

TWO

A CASE FOR
THE COLLEGE BOY

The general public has a deathly fear of large caliber pistols. That is understandable, but somewhat misinformed. You see, a small gun firing small bullets can cause much more physical harm than a monstrous Dirty Harry .44 Magnum revolver that fires cannonballs. A big bullet punches a hole through the body. If it doesn't hit anything important along its path, you just put a Band-Aid on the entry and exit holes and you're pretty much out of danger.

A small-caliber bullet can do much more damage because it ricochets around the victim's body, taking the grand tour. This greatly multiplies the danger of damage to vital organs and major arteries. Think of it as death by a thousand cuts. The victim might hang on to life for a day or two, but often the result is a premature departure to the hereafter.

Homicide detectives know this all too well because they don't get fully involved until a bullet or some other killing tool proves lethal. That's why I was able to step in and take a small-caliber case that had a major impact on my career.

CHASING THE GOLD AT 7-ELEVEN

After three years as a patrolman, I was promoted to burglary detective, which was a step in the right direction, but only a step. I wanted a homicide detective badge. Burglary detectives wear a flimsier metal alloy badge. When I got mine, my brothers in blue upgraded me from "Shit Magnet" patrolman to a "Pewter Badge Puke" member of the burglary squad.

I was honored, but by no means placated. I still wanted to hunt bigger game. Investigating burglaries was like playing Trivial Pursuit, in my mind. Most burglary victims are insured against loss of property. I'm not minimizing that they are crime victims. It can be very disturbing to have a stranger go through your personal things. They might feel violated and fearful that their security was breached, but nobody died.

On top of that, burglars typically get probation, because there isn't room in the overwhelmed prison system for them, so even when you catch the perpetrator, you don't get the satisfaction of putting away the bad guy for a long time. I wanted to take killers off the street permanently. There is great satisfaction in that.

Fortunately, I was in burglary for less than a year when I seized upon the case that brought me a coveted detective badge. This game-changer was an armed robbery in which two victims were seriously wounded, but skillful doctors stabilized them quickly. Still, they were on the precipice of death, so this one appeared likely to become a murder case—and one with some special challenges.

I was called to the scene initially only because it was an all-hands-on-deck situation. A female clerk and a male customer had been shot by a small-caliber handgun during an armed robbery at a 7-Eleven convenience store in a densely populated neighborhood.

The bad guy fled the scene. We had not a clue to his identity. The store was surrounded by apartment buildings, so there were a lot of potential witnesses who had to be interviewed. Thus the call went out for all available personnel, even the burglary detectives.

When I arrived, the front door of the store was propped open for the ambulance gurneys. Nobody was guarding it so I walked in like it was my job. A bold move, I know, but crime scenes call to me. I figured a quick look would help me when questioning potential witnesses. Also, I am a competitive SOB and I was fired up. I wanted to solve the case. I *always* want to solve the case.

On my tour of the ravaged 7-Eleven, I tried to visualize what had happened and how the armed robber and his prey had behaved. I immersed myself in the crime scene.

Just as I entered a zone, my sleuthing was rudely interrupted.

"Hey, Kenda, what the fuck are you doing in there? Get out!"

Yelling at me was not really effective when I was in the flow. My brain and all my senses were focused on reading the crime scene. I was extended another invitation to evacuate, but I made one last, long scan before departing with it imprinted on my brain.

The store was a mess. Signs of a major knock-down, drag-out fight. Blood on the floor. Displays knocked over. Canned goods, cereal boxes, and other items strewn everywhere. All of this was to be expected based on what had happened there.

Mayhem had occurred, possibly murder. A convenience store turned upside down, but a convenience store with all the usual items. Except one. A metal display rack that had contained family-sized potato chip bags had been dumped over. The chip bags were scattered on the floor, but among them, lying under the lowest shelf of a nearby display case, was an ID bracelet, a linked chain with a flat piece of metal that was not polished silver, but smoke-colored.

These bracelets were very common in the late 1970s. Boyfriends gave them to their girlfriends. Girlfriends gave them to their boyfriends. Romance on the cheap.

I didn't know if this one came from a customer who'd lost it or one of the shooting victims, or their attacker. The piece of chintzy jewelry amid all the scattered grocery goods intrigued me. I didn't pick it up because the bracelet was physical evidence that should be left for the crime scene guys to examine, bag, and catalog. I did store an image of the bracelet in my mind's own evidence locker after mentally labeling it "potentially useful."

A LOSER CASE

I stepped outside. A dumpy homicide sergeant was handing out addresses in the surrounding neighborhood, assigning them to all of us dragged in to help knock on doors. This was early on a Sunday morning. Most residents, other than avid churchgoers, were still tucked in their beds. It was unlikely that anyone had been awakened by the small-caliber handgun being shot inside a brick building.

Still, there were a lot of people living nearby. Maybe some of them were insomniacs with excellent hearing, or curious sorts looking out the right window at the right time. I hit the street, awakening the public to a violent crime in their midst. Everyone was surprised. No one had heard gunshots. No one had seen the suspect enter or flee.

After a couple of hours of banging my head against a dense wall, I rejoined my fellow officers and reported back to the homicide sergeant, who crossed off addresses one by one as they were cleared. I was standing in line to offer my own lack of success when I overheard the grumblings and wheezing of several overweight veteran detectives. The old limp dicks were moaning and groaning that the 7-Eleven case was a loser. Nobody wanted to be assigned to it.

Their expert summation: a random robbery, hit-and-run shooting, no likely links between the victims and the bad guy. They also noted that since both victims were still breathing, this wasn't a homicide. They were backing away from this one like it was a rabid skunk.

Their homicide sergeant wasn't unsympathetic. He seemed to see the case as a loser, too.

As I observed this, my competitive juices roiled. I was young and aggressive and, as you might suspect, not adept at keeping my mouth shut.

"Hey, I'll take this case if no one wants it."

Oh, sweet Jesus, did I say that out loud?

The homicide sergeant at first glared at me. Then he smirked as his oafish pack of detectives mocked me: "Yeah, Sarge, give it to the college boy. He'll have it solved before recess!"

I waited for their smirking leader to tell me where to shove it. Then he surprised me.

"Let me see if your sergeant will approve that, Kenda. If he does, you can have it," he said, silencing his boys.

Maybe the homicide sergeant wanted to see me fall on my face. Maybe he secretly hoped I'd show up the old guard. More likely, he just wanted to hand off this "loser" case while he still could.

The next day, he dropped the file on my desk and said it was mine. Both victims were still hanging on so the case was in limbo anyway. My initial thought was, *Oh my God, what have I done? I just put my career on the line. If this comes up snake eyes, I'll be investigating VCR heists until I die.*

Then I had another thought: *Nothing ventured. Nothing gained.*

A BIG GULP

Once they gave me the 7-Eleven case, I became a man on a mission. Food, water, and sleep were unnecessary distractions. This shooter was mine. He just didn't know it yet.

My first stop was the hospital. Store clerk Susan Irving, who'd been shot in the forehead, was hanging on to her nineteenth year of life. Normally cops aren't allowed to interview victims in intensive care. So I tried not to look like a cop. I was wearing a nice suit, bought off-season at a discount. I assumed a physician's confident manner. Apparently acting was in my future.

"Good morning, Doctor," said a nurse.

I went with that.

"Good morning, nurse," I said.

I didn't say I was a doctor. She did.

Susan Irving's head was swathed in bandages. A respirator was keeping her alive. She looked awful. I felt sad for her, then angry, then vengeful.

None of the nurses paid attention to me. They wandered away, thinking I was on the hospital staff. I stepped up to the bed. As I looked down at her, Miss Irving shot up to a sitting position, ripped the respirator mask from her face, and screamed like a zombie banshee.

My entire body puckered. Someone had vacuum-packed my vital organs. My heart blew a rod. A nurse approached as I stood frozen solid.

Obviously, I was not a trained medical professional.

"Get out, whoever you are," she commanded.

Miss Irving would not be available for an interview, though a real doctor confirmed that she was still alive. Relieved that I hadn't somehow killed my first witness, I skulked down the hall to post-op, looking for the other 7-Eleven shooting victim, a sixty-three-year-old rancher who'd gone to buy his Sunday paper and bought a bullet instead.

This time I didn't try to play Marcus Welby, M.D. I found a real physician, identified myself as a detective, and asked if I could speak with Mr. Fred Howard, a gunshot victim recovering from surgery.

The doctor said he was doped up and probably incoherent, but he let me give it a shot.

"Don't stay too long," the doctor said.

Fred Howard was awake, and groggy, but just coherent enough to explain to me what happened. He'd gone to the convenience store to buy the *Rocky Mountain News* at 7 a.m. He wasn't planning to go inside. There was a newspaper vending machine out front.

While feeding it quarters, he saw a guy open the front door of the store and gesture at him to come inside. "Hey buddy, come in here. There is a girl hurt."

My guess is the bad guy lured him in because he thought Mr. Howard saw him through the window. He didn't. He was focused on buying his paper.

Mr. Howard went inside, being the Good Samaritan. The guy pointed behind the sales counter, where poor Susan Irving was lying in a puddle of blood.

"That's when I got a really bad feeling," Howard told me from his hospital bed.

He turned around to find a handgun aimed between his eyes at close range. He threw his hands up in front of his face just as the bad guy pulled the trigger. A churchgoing person might say divine intervention stepped in at that moment. The bullet struck the wedding ring on his finger, blowing the ring and the finger off, but saving Mr. Howard from a lethal shot to the face.

The rancher then fought for his life. He and the shooter locked up and wrestled through the store, tearing up the place. The robber was younger and more muscular, but Mr. Howard was tough as old leather. The struggle went on until the robber fired four more shots into the rancher's chest. He went down.

The robber fled, taking all of thirty-one dollars in cash.

Both victims were lucky to still be alive when the paramedics arrived. I was admiring the old guy's tenacity when he offered up a piece of information that made me even more fond of him.

"While we were fighting, I pulled an ID bracelet off his wrist," he said. "I don't know where we were, but I ripped it off his arm and it went flying."

I told him I'd seen it on the floor of the store, and I'd be sure to check it out.

Then I asked if he could describe the shooter.

"I think he was a white guy," he said.

His voice was weak. He was fading in and out. I thanked him and told him I'd be back. Before I left, he opened his eyes and whispered: "Find him."

"I will," I promised.

I will get this son of a bitch or die in the attempt, I thought.

AN ID BRACELET THAT DID ITS JOB

My next stop was the evidence room back at the station. I asked for everything from the 7-Eleven crime scene. The box contained casings from a .25-caliber handgun, a Saturday night special. I was not surprised. This was probably a Raven P25, the cheap weapon of choice for low-rent criminals everywhere.

Made by Raven Arms out of Southern California, it is small and easy to conceal, a piece of junk that holds seven rounds. A new one cost less than a hundred bucks so there are a lot of them out there. The .25 bullet casings would tell me only so much.

The ID bracelet offered much more potential. I found it inside a brown manila envelope, which I took into my office for closer study. *Talk to me.*

When I examined it closely, I saw for the first time that there was a name on the plate: "Ingrid." A German name. This did not surprise me. The local joke was that there were more Germans in Colorado Springs than in Berlin. The town had three major military bases. Soldiers often do a tour in Germany. Many of them marry German girls, which is why the Springs had so many hofbrau bars, bratwurst delis, and hearty blue-eyed blondes.

It was plausible that my shooter had worn the ID bracelet bearing the name of his girl Ingrid. Perhaps she'd purchased it for him in our fair city. My restless mind took that and ran with it, of course. He could have bought it just as easily in Denver or even Dusseldorf, but I decided to start locally. Our police department didn't have much of a travel budget anyway.

I stared at the bracelet. I poked it with my pen. *Speak to me. Give me your secrets.*

Not a word. I turned it over and stared at the "Ingrid" engraving. The bracelet seemed cheaply made, but the engraving was fancy, almost three dimensional. I thought it was cooler than most I'd seen, and maybe unique.

Unique would be helpful. I took the bracelet for a ride to Bowie's Gold & Diamonds, a fixture in the Springs since the early 1960s. Mr. Bowie had helped me out on other burglary cases involving stolen jewelry. He was rarely surprised, as well as highly accurate.

He was also very frank in his appraisals.

"It's junk," he said. "A four-dollar item. I don't sell junk like that."

I tipped the bracelet so he could see the engraving.

"Is this style of engraving unusual?" I asked.

He put on his jeweler's loupe with a magnifying lens to get a better look.

"Yes, it is," he said, to my delight.

"There is only one machine that can make that double cut. It's made by Hermes Engraving in Connecticut. I was thinking about buying one. A lot of stores have them these days."

Finally, a promising lead. I called Hermes headquarters and asked for the names of places in Colorado Springs that had purchased their double-cut engraving machines. They kept sales records because their machines come with warranties. Hermes said they'd check and get back to me. The next day, they called with a list of fifty-nine places around town. I asked them to mail the list.

We didn't have email or fax machines back then so everything took longer.

Three weeks dragged by before I had the list in my hands. I hit the streets, first checking the stores closest to the 7-Eleven location. Nothing turned up. So, I worked my way through the others. I was hoping that whoever had sold and engraved the ID bracelet would remember the "Ingrid" customer and maybe have a receipt with an address.

CAN-DO SPIRIT

It's a good thing I'm a patient and persevering man. The first twenty-six places had nothing for me. I had burned through the list and I was running out of gas. My twenty-seventh stop was the Can-Do Shop, which was little more than a booth in the Citadel Mall. The shop repaired and sold cheap watches and jewelry. They catered to impulse buyers with low budgets.

The Citadel was the new big mall in town back then, and very popular, drawing from all over the area. I arrived shortly after it opened. I wasn't so much eager as desperate. My wife and friends were beginning to wonder about me and my fixation with the 7-Eleven case. Why was this one so important to me?

The salesgirl in the mall shop said she worked nearly every day. She recognized the ID bracelet as one of their items. I turned it over and displayed the "Ingrid" engraving.

"Do you recognize this?"

"Oh yeah!" she said.

I almost dropped my notebook.

"You do?"

"Yeah, the guy was a total asshole!"

Well, I just might be looking for one of those.

"Can you tell me his name?"

"I never knew his name," she said. "He was a black guy with

this German girl. She wanted him to buy the ID bracelet and wear it, but all he did was complain that it was too expensive. The bracelet was four dollars. The engraving charge was two dollars. But all he did was complain and demand a discount."

The salesgirl said the strange thing was that the German woman, who was a very pretty lady, put up with the loud-mouth asshole. "It was as if he was some kind of god to her," she said.

After much discussion, she said, the guy paid up with cash. The salesclerk wrote a receipt with Ingrid's name and address. She handed it to Ingrid, along with the thirty-day warranty. The salesgirl then put a pink carbon copy of the receipt in her receipt drawer.

This had all happened a couple of weeks earlier. I asked the salesgirl if she still had the receipt. She pulled out her big box with the month's sales receipts in it. There were at least nine hundred pieces of pink copy paper. Each was three inches long and four inches wide.

ONE CLUE LEADS TO ANOTHER

Company policy did not allow for me to take the whole box back to my office. She did let me take it to a quiet service corridor in the mall. I sat on a stair step and pored through the contents. Faded pink carbon copies are not the easiest things to eyeball quickly. I had to examine each one, carefully, blinking to clear my eyes, hoping the name Ingrid would jump out at me.

As closing time at the mall drew near, I'd only made it about two-thirds of the way through the contents of the box. The salesgirl stared at me nervously.

I was feeling a little guilty, until I found it.

Got you, Ingrid!

The receipt had her name and an apartment address on the West Side, about ten miles from the mall, but not so far from the 7-Eleven. I had assumed the armed robber/asshole lived near the convenience store. That's usually the case with small-time crooks. They rob close by so they have limited exposure on the street while hightailing it home. There is rarely a getaway car. Most of them walk or run.

I had Ingrid's address, a big lead, but I didn't go to talk to her right away. I didn't want to set off alarms and spook the boyfriend. Instead, I did a drive-by in an unmarked car. She had a small ground-level place in what looked like an old motel that had been converted into apartments. It was a long, straight building with a yard and sidewalks.

There were houses across the street. I knocked on their doors. Wearing a sport coat, tie, and slacks, I could have been a door-to-door insurance salesman if Ingrid spotted me from her place.

A lady answered at a house directly across the street. I discreetly showed my badge.

"Do you know who lives in that apartment right there?"

"That's Ingrid," she said. "She seems nice. She works during the day."

"Does anybody else live there? Like a boyfriend?" I asked.

"I think she dates, but I've never seen anyone there with her."

This was all good. Ingrid still lived at the address. It seemed she lived alone. She worked days, so she should be home at night. That's probably when the boyfriend came around, which explains why the neighbor lady had not seen him.

I planned to do a night surveillance on the apartment. First, I wanted to learn more about Ingrid and her boyfriend. I went back to the police records department. I asked the clerk, a cranky former patrol cop, to dig out every incident report in the immediate vicinity of Ingrid's building. I told him to check reports over the last couple of months.

"What the fuck do you want all that for? Do you know how long that will take?" said the surly clerk.

"What else do you have to do?" I asked.

He was an example of why cops get assigned to low-level desk jobs—because they deserve them. My reason for asking for incident reports in that area was simple: The guy I was looking for was a serial asshole. That's been established both at the convenience store and at the mall shop. He was also a violent criminal. Established rules meant nothing to him. It was likely that he'd run afoul of the law more than once. I was hoping he had done it near Ingrid's place.

Maybe a speeding ticket. Maybe a confrontation over a parking space. Maybe indecent exposure for pissing on the sidewalk. I was looking for any records that could give me a name. The records search burned up another day.

A PARKING TICKET TO PRISON

Finally, I received a long printout that was faded and hard to read. The only thing that caught my eye was a parking ticket for a car in a space on the street directly in front of Ingrid's apartment. Someone had parked a white, two-door Oldsmobile, a piece-of-crap eight-hundred-dollar car, facing the wrong way, against traffic flow. Only a person who doesn't give a fuck would do that. An asshole.

Perhaps *my* suspect asshole?

The ticket was issued at 1 a.m. It hadn't been paid. The officer who wrote the citation had checked the vehicle's registration. Like a good cop, he wrote down the name of the owner. Fred Henry Swain.

Well, there you are, Freddy. Got you! You cocksucker.

Sorry, I didn't mean to write that out loud.

I checked Freddy's criminal history. No surprise: His jacket had page after page of armed robbery and weapons complaints. He'd done time for both. He had just returned to the street after a prison hitch.

Freddy was looking like the right guy. The criminal history

also offered his mug shots, front and side views. He was a good-looking guy, a prison bodybuilder. I'm sure Ingrid thought he was wonderful.

I put together a photo lineup featuring Freddy and friends he didn't know he had. This is similar to a physical lineup when you bring in witnesses to view several individuals of similar appearance, one of whom is usually the primary suspect.

A photo lineup takes less time and organization. You just put together six mug shots. You have the witness sign a form that says you made it clear that the suspect may or may not be among those in the photos. Then you ask if the witness recognizes anyone.

"That's the asshole right there," said the still-offended Can-Do salesclerk.

"Are you sure?"

"I am as sure as God made me," she said. "That's him!"

I didn't walk out of the Citadel Mall. I floated. I was euphoric.

After a brief moment of celebration, I reined in my euphoria. *Don't jump the gun. Another eyewitness confirmation would be useful.* I went back to Mr. Howard, who was still in the hospital but easing off the painkillers. I showed him the same photo lineup.

He picked out Fred Swain, too.

One problem with that, however.

"When I talked to you earlier, you said he was white," I said.

"Well, I was fucked up from my operation then," he said. "That's him."

CLOSING IN

I wrote up a request for an arrest warrant and the judge granted it. That night, armed with the signed warrant, I recruited another detective and two patrol officers to stake out the apartment with me. We didn't want a raging gun battle. We preferred to trap Freddy alone in a contained area. The plan was to catch him in his car as he drove up, box him in with our squads, and cut off any escape.

We set up and waited. The longest hour of my life. I chain-smoked an entire pack of cigarettes before Freddy's white wreck came around the corner. A female was in the passenger seat. We assumed it was the lovely Ingrid.

Freddy parked legally this time. It didn't matter. Our two squad cars rolled up and blocked the Olds so it couldn't go anywhere. We were on top of him with guns drawn before he could make an ass-hole move. We ordered him out of his car.

This was not Freddy's first arrest. His hands went right up. A local news photographer, who'd been intrigued by the case and tipped about the potential bust, snapped away. The dramatic photo of young Detective Kenda cuffing the sneering 7-Eleven shooter with a patrolman pointing a gun at him made the front page. The photographer won a news photography prize for it.

Ingrid, an attractive young woman with a blond Afro, put up a little fuss over the arrest, but we paid no attention. She wasn't on our radar anymore. I later learned, as I'd suspected, that she didn't know about the 7-Eleven robbery or Freddy's many other crimes. She'd met him in a bar and started sleeping with him without even knowing his last name. He lived in his own place two blocks from the convenience store. We searched his apartment and found his Raven P25 stuffed under a mattress, where no one would ever look.

Five days after I had come up with his name from the park-ing ticket, I walked Freddy into the station for booking. The homi-cide detectives who'd run away from the case couldn't believe I'd nabbed the guy. To his credit, one of them who had relentlessly teased me said, "Good job, for a college boy."

So, at age twenty-nine, I earned a new nickname, and a new job with a homicide detective's badge. I also came away feeling like I'd made the right career choice. I felt I could be successful. I proved that my instincts were good, which was all that mattered. Sure, I'd had moments during the investigation when I had to stop and center myself to keep from feeling overwhelmed. I'd controlled my emotions and relied on my understanding of human nature. I'd read the shooter as someone who thought the standard rules of law didn't apply to him and I'd been right.

For the rest of my career, I followed essentially the same methodology of looking at a crime scene, putting myself in the mind of the perpetrator, and asking questions: *What did you do here? Why did you do it? What was your first move? What was next?* I always tried to understand the person and the behavior and then I tried to get a feel for the personality and type of individual I was looking for. Getting excited never helped. I'd calm myself, put my hands in my pockets, and made myself relax. *Let's just see what's going on here.*

Later in my career, I coached younger detectives to do the same thing. One of my young detectives went running past me at a violent-crime scene one night. I called out to him, "Come here and talk to me."

He was frantic. Everyone was frantic.

"Did you commit this crime?" I asked him. "Did you kill the victim?"

"Well, no," he said.

"Then why are you so upset? Put a paper bag over your head and breathe until you calm yourself. I need your brain to be engaged."

A RANCHER'S REVENGE

Of course, once an arrest has been made and reports are written, the case moves through the judicial system and anything can happen. Freddy, good citizen that he was, pleaded not guilty and sought a trial by his peers under our judicial system. Despite his best efforts to kill two innocent people, he was not facing murder charges. Susan Irving and Fred Howard had managed to remain alive, so the accused was facing multiple charges including attempted murder.

The asshole had his day in court. There was a potential weak spot in the prosecution's case. My report on my initial post-op interview with the still-groggy rancher noted that he had identified his shooter as a white man.

As expected, the defense attorney homed in on that point. He was all over it, as would be expected. He was doing his job. Well, mostly. You see, he had neglected to interview Fred Howard before the trial. He didn't know who he was dealing with, or what the tough ol' guy would say when poked with a stick.

That was a terrible mistake.

"Mr. Howard, isn't it true, sir, that when Detective Kenda first interviewed you, you told him that the person who shot you was a white male?"

"Well, I probably did tell him that," said Mr. Howard, looking like *Chisum* John Wayne on the stand.

The defense attorney then went into his best Bombastic Bushkin courtroom interrogation routine.

"Well, as you can see, sir, my client is a black male!"

The defense attorney surveyed the jury in triumph. He seemed to think he'd just won his case.

But Mr. Howard was still on the stand and he wasn't done.

"Let me tell you something, Mr. Lawyer. I don't know what I told that detective the first time because I was pretty hurting. But when somebody tries to kill you, you remember him—and it was that [blank] right there!"

The blank reflects that Mr. Howard used a racial epithet that I won't repeat here. If you want to know what it was, you can check the official court record. The faces of the jury made it clear that they believed Mr. Howard. Their deliberations were so swift that as the last juror left the jury box the first one was coming back in. (That's an old courthouse joke, but it is also true for this case.)

The judge gave Freddy ninety-nine years with no chance for parole. He will die in prison. Fred Howard, the rancher, lived another ten years after being shot five times. Susan Irving was left paralyzed and, sadly, lived only a few years after being shot in the robbery.

I have not forgotten her, or Mr. Howard, or any of the murder victims I sought to avenge. They will always be with me.

THREE

TOO REAL FOR REALITY TV

Picture yourself on a cliff looking out onto the Serengeti Plain of Africa nearly two million years ago. Roving herds and packs of mammals of all types populate the grasslands. Many are huge predators with razor claws and flesh-shredding teeth set in powerful jaws. You instinctively know to avoid them.

The least intimidating creature within your view is a slight, five-foot-tall *Homo erectus*, covered in hair and walking in a crouch, yet upright on two legs. This is early man, a cunning carnivore who uses crude tools and makes odd guttural sounds to communicate with members of his tribe.

You wonder at first how this relatively frail mammal survives amid so many bigger, stronger, and faster beasts. Then you note that he lives and hunts in packs, carries weapons, and appears to use his wiles to capture and kill much larger prey. Slowly it dawns on you that man is deadlier than predators three or four times its size.

Most other mammals learned to keep a safe distance from early man for those reasons. Even today, humans are the most ruthless, aggressive, and dangerous of species. Many have hair-trigger tempers driven by rage. Modern man may have evolved over the centuries, but those most primitive instincts can and do surface. They can overpower and bury even a parent's natural empathy and compassion for a child.

I was working the day shift when a West Sider called in to report possible child abuse by a neighbor. A single mother was leaving her six-year-old home alone while she went to work each day. No one else ever showed up to look after the child.

I was still a patrolman with my own squad car. I went to the house, a wretched little cottage, maybe nine hundred square feet total, that sorely needed painting. It was summer. The front door was open, but the screen behind it was hooked shut.

I knocked. No answer. I then hit the side of the house with my nightstick. This is known as the "police knock" and it can wake the dead.

From the dark interior of the house a little voice squeaked out a fearful "Hello?"

"Hi, I'm a policeman. Can you come to the door?"

"No."

"Why not?"

"Mommy chained me to the bed."

I kicked the screen door off its hinges. Inside a bedroom, I found an emaciated six-year-old with thick scar tissue under the dog collar around his neck. The chain on the collar was secured to a leg of the bed.

He rubbed his neck when I freed him, and I gave him a hug. Then I called everybody and his brother in social services to come get the child and take him away for good.

I couldn't get to mommy's place of employment fast enough. I spun her around, cuffed her, and arrested her for felony child abuse. When she turned back around, I told her that I was hoping she would resist arrest, but then again, she probably didn't try to hurt anyone who was big enough to fight back.

I told her that if it was in my power I would have gladly shoved a gun in her mouth and pulled the trigger for what she'd done to her child, but since my supervisors frowned on that, I hauled her ass off to jail.

She cried all the way, this scrawny woman working a menial job. She had to work and couldn't afford child care so she chained her kid to the bed. Like there were no other options.

After you see a few of these cases you realize maternal instincts can be highly overrated. Motherhood doesn't mean shit as far as what some degenerates will do to their offspring. That's very disappointing to learn, but it's all too common.

NOT READY FOR PRIME TIME

These cases involving cruelty or the deaths of children are among those that I can't talk about on television because they are simply too heinous and distressing for a general viewing audience. Frankly, they always hit me hard, too. Kids are just so vulnerable. Most of the cases that still torment me involved children. Some have lingered longer than others.

We got a call from the Los Angeles Police Department looking for a gang guy running from a contract killing in their jurisdiction. They said he had a girlfriend in Colorado Springs and might show up in our town. They sent photos of him and gave us her address. We set up surveillance on her crummy little apartment. He showed up. We did not rush in.

LAPD had warned us that he was armed and dangerous. I asked a judge for a no-knock warrant, which would allow our tactical team to blow through the door with a show of overwhelming force. We hit the door with a plastic explosive charge that blew it out, not in. Then we tossed in "flash-bang" grenades. Imagine an incredibly loud Fourth of July fireworks show in your living room. It's designed to temporarily blind and disable the bad guys.

Chaos ensued, according to plan. The noise, flash, and smoke left the gangbanger so disoriented, he couldn't get his gun out of his pants. We put him down while he screamed that he'd kill us all and his 350-pound girlfriend shrieked at us. I began searching the apartment as the smoke cleared. Then I saw the boy.

He was no more than four or five, standing at the top of the stairs, shaking uncontrollably. He'd wet his pants. I went up the stairs and knelt in front of him.

"It's okay, son, nobody is going to hurt you," I said. "You are safe now."

He hugged me with the strength of an adult. His arms were still locked around me when his mother came pounding up the stairs.

"Get your motherfuckin' hands off my baby!" she screamed.

A member of the tactical team ran up the stairs to secure her and drag her away. She'd been harboring a fugitive. She was headed for prison and her poor scared child was going to social services. I gave him one last hug and cleared the scene.

I could still feel his arms around me as I sat in my unmarked car, shaking. The poor innocent kid, so scared and now, so alone because the adults in his life failed him so miserably.

One X-ray One! One X-ray One!

A dispatcher was calling me on the car's police radio. I ignored her as I grieved over the kid, his fear and the hopelessness of the future he faced.

One X-ray One! One X-ray One!

The dispatcher sounded pissed, like a wife being ignored. She knew I was in the car because I'd cleared from the apartment.

One X-ray One. Respond to a body found at . . .

The dead wouldn't wait. They were piling up in the streets. Time to close the door on the kid and his pain, for now.

Back to work.

This is One X-ray One . . .

CROSSING THE LINE

The network that airs our show is in the entertainment business, and while shocking viewers to a certain extent is acceptable, we all agree that there is no need to sicken them, provoke nightmares, or send them fleeing to a mellower *Murder, She Wrote* episode on another channel. We have pushed the line occasionally on the show, and our viewers have not been shy about complaining.

The episode that stirred a lot of revulsion featured a victim who died of "blue-eyed asphyxia" at the hands of his drunken and enraged drinking companion, a woman nearly forty years younger than him. They were both thoroughly drunk, hanging out in an abandoned building and fighting over a bottle of vodka. She got pissed and violent. To her friend's misfortune, somewhere she had learned an extreme street-fighting technique, usually taught as a last-ditch self-defense move.

She had apparently learned it quite well.

A security guard found them side by side in a dark and squalid spot and called us. She was passed out drunk. He was just dead. Oddly, there were no apparent wounds on his body. No weapon nearby. In the shadows, I didn't notice until I leaned down that there was something wrong with his eyes.

I pulled back one eyelid and there was no eyeball. The other eye socket was vacant, too. Some weird voodoo ritual? Santeria, maybe?

My search for a motive was interrupted when I noticed something jammed in the victim's mouth. I parted his lips and a blue eyeball stared out at me.

Oh, hello! You are in the wrong place, Mr. Eyeball.

She had popped out both his eyeballs with her thumbs and then taken her depravity a step further, shoving both into his mouth. The second jammed into his windpipe. The victim choked to death on his own eye lodged in his airway.

Yeah, that was pushing the envelope for a prime-time television audience. I saw one viewer comment that the episode made her gag even though she'd been a nurse for thirty years. I'm pretty sure the comment wasn't written by my wife, but she had much the same reaction.

Another episode that created angst among the Legions of Decency involved a woman whose husband had come into the station and reported her missing. The veteran cop who took the report came to me with a JDLR— that is cop-speak for *Just Doesn't Look Right*. His instincts were on target. We interviewed the husband and agreed something was off with his story. He claimed he and his wife went to their separate jobs one day and she never came home. He found her car parked at her workplace, but no sign of her.

We looked at the car. Her purse, with cash, credit cards, and her ID, was locked in it, as was her habit. We interrogated the husband again. We weren't as sympathetic this time. He wilted and then folded.

He'd strangled her on a trout fishing trip at a state-owned hatchery up in the mountains over Colorado Springs. His wife thought he should get a second job to help support her parents instead of wasting his time fishing. He disagreed.

It was a long-running feud. He ended it by strangling her.

So far, none of this is too shocking, but then it took a turn—one that we did not include on our televised depiction. We had the husband's confession, but we didn't have her body, which we needed to prosecute him for murder. A confession does not fulfill the burden of proof. We needed a body.

The now-repentant spouse killer had confessed late at night. We told him he needed to take us to the spot where he'd left his victim. He described it as remote, so we requisitioned a fire department truck equipped with a battery of floodlights.

The husband directed us to a remote area on State Road 115,

between Cheyenne Mountain Air Force Base and Fort Carson. He'd dumped her in a ditch along the two-lane to Cañon City.

We get to the sparse location and hit the floodlights. Midnight turns to midday at the flick of a switch. We see nothing but sagebrush. No body. No blood. No clothing or shoes.

"I'm tired and hungry, don't fuck with me," I say. "Where is your old lady?"

"I don't know. I'm telling you, I dumped her here two days ago," he answers.

He seems truly shocked. I'm truly pissed. We head back, still without proof of death.

The next morning, we learn that a resident of an affluent neighborhood on the very southwestern edge of town has called in a relevant report. He'd turned his Labrador retriever out for the morning and the dog did what retrievers do. Except this wasn't a duck or a goose. It was the severely mangled head of an Asian lady, which matched the general description of our missing murder victim.

A squad had already picked up the head and taken it to the morgue, after rewarding the Lab with a few pats on the head. We went to the morgue. The head was mauled beyond recognition, but the teeth were intact. Later we received a positive ID from the victim's dental records.

Since the husband had not confessed to beheading the wife, and the damage was so severe, we presumed "wild animal interference" might be a factor. (Labs are known for their soft mouths, so the dog was not a suspect.) We called in a wildlife expert, warning him that this would not be a pleasant experience.

He took one look and went into severe hyperventilation. We got him to a chair before he passed out. After we had revived him with two unfiltered cups of coffee, he offered an expert assessment.

"That damage was done by a bear," he said. "I have no doubt."

Rocky Mountain black bears have always been plentiful in

that area. They are omnivorous. The bear got away. The husband got forty-eight years.

MAN'S INHUMANITY TO MEN, WOMEN, AND CHILDREN

I was never surprised, but often disappointed. The vicious things that people were capable of doing to spouses, children, friends, and strangers often made me wonder about the true nature of the human race. We claim that our ability to reason makes us superior to other mammals. I don't think so. There was no reasoning involved for many of the murders I witnessed.

Crime scenes often resembled normal, happy homes. We'd go into a house and walk past walls of wedding, birthday, and anniversary photos. Everyone looking happy. Men and their wives hugging, kissing, looking blissful.

Then we'd come upon the bloody mess in the family room. If you think it's a little extreme to kill your spouse because she doesn't approve of your love of fishing, please think again. Minor marital disputes often turn into the messiest of murders, in my experience. I only had about an hour remaining in my shift one night when my phone rang, interrupting my paperwork.

"Is this homicide?"

"Why yes, it is. How can I help?"

"You'd better come over to my house."

"Why is that, sir?"

"Because I killed my wife."

I rounded up three other detectives and we headed over to the address he thoughtfully provided. We found his wife with a .30-06 caliber bullet entrance wound in her sternum. The former contents of her chest cavity were splattered on the wall behind her. The street cop description of this sort of wound is, "It went in like a dime and came out like a cash register."

The weapon used was a deer rifle. She appeared to have been dead three or four hours, which left a considerable gap before the husband called in his report. He calmly admitted that he'd taken his time.

"Here's the deal, I love to watch *Monday Night Football*. My wife hates football. She wants to watch some stupid show that she likes. We have been fighting over this for years. She started in tonight and we got into it. I said, 'Fuck it,' grabbed my rifle, and killed that bitch. Then I watched the game before I called you."

Evidence suggested that he hadn't considered simply going to a sports bar—they have beer, burgers, hot chicken wings, and often cute waitresses. Nor did he opt for the civil thing by hiring a divorce attorney. I'm sure those options became more attractive once his cell mate informed him that there is no *Monday Night Football* in prison.

ABUSE OF INNOCENTS

Someone wise once said that the unpredictable nature of human behavior is widely known. I agree with that statement. Humans are capable of incredible cruelty against each other, including their young. If you work in law enforcement, emergency medicine, and other fields that expose you to the harshest aspects of life and death, none of these tales will surprise you.

Even the most seasoned cops, EMTs, social workers, and medical professionals will tell you that witnessing the abuse of innocents is probably the most difficult aspect of their work. That is the ultimate evil, in my mind. I wanted to hurt those abusers like they hurt the kids, who were often the same ages as my own son and daughter.

Many nights I went home after work and hugged them. They had no idea why.

"What's going on, Dad?"

Kathy had no questions. As a nurse, she knew.

The sound of a crying child stirs compassion from most of us, certainly if the kid is our own. Yet there are those who don't share the compassion gene, or they have been numbed to it. Instead they are annoyed or even driven to violence by the same innocent cries.

I arrested a guy who had that reaction in the extreme. He was not the father. The child belonged to his girlfriend. Still, that doesn't explain the vicious rage that compelled him to grab the two-year-old girl by her ankles and swing her into a wall as if she were a baseball bat.

When I arrived, he tried to convince me that she had sustained her massive fatal injuries by falling off the sofa.

"Only if the sofa was located on the edge of the observation deck of the Empire State Building," I said.

Usually child abusers are incapable of conceptual thought. The mother who chained her son to the bed, for example, had not evolved beyond survival mode. This particular neglected child underwent medical treatment for quite a long time before going into foster care. He was never returned to his worthless mother. She went to prison for felony child abuse.

She was among those women who never should have been allowed to conceive children, because they lack maternal instincts, mental clarity, and, probably, souls. This also describes a nineteen-year-old public-housing resident in Colorado Springs who came under my scrutiny when she went to her fast-food job and left her thirteen-month-old son in the care of a mentally-disabled thirty-year-old whose only qualification was that he lived in the same complex.

Her child care on the cheap plan went just fine for a couple of months, as far as we know. We weren't called until the day the unfit mother came home to find her child's caregiver highly frustrated. The toddler was in his high chair but wouldn't take food from the babysitter.

When she checked, she found her son stabbed to death with a kitchen knife.

UNFIT TO PARENT

The right-to-life people talk about bringing all the unwanted babies into the world. Then they go home after their protests, scheduled for their convenience. Police officers are left to deal with the aftermath of their righteous cause. I'd like to see all the unwanted babies brought to the homes of the right-to-life people. We'll bring you 1,200 babies on Monday. You can feed and nourish them and send them to college. The next week we will bring you 1,200 more. That is the reality of the right-to-life equation. Nobody wants to think about it, but it is the way things are in this world. Unwanted children suffer.

People behave badly, and this includes even those who you'd think would know better. My wife worked with another RN, an educated person with a good job, who cared for newborns in the hospital nursery. Meanwhile, she left her own child at home in a crib for her entire eight-hour shift. She didn't want to pay a babysitter. The child survived, no thanks to the mother.

Crazy people don't know any better, but these two mothers are among those who should. They take the "easy" way out to avoid complications in their lives, so they treat their children like dogs. Does the mother think that a child chained to a bed and abandoned will grow up to be just fine? I don't think so. An abused and neglected child becomes an abusive adult. They treat their children just as they were treated.

Many child killings are the result of a parent or adult guardian "disciplining" a child to extremes. They punch too hard, choke too much, throw the child down too forcefully, or restrain them to death. The intent may not be murder, but that is the result.

I obtained many confessions from child murderers in the

interrogation room by putting a hand on the shoulder and whispering in the ear: "I know you didn't mean to kill this child. Tell me what happened."

TOO CLOSE TO HOME

In some cases, there is no suspect to interrogate because the killer has taken the easy way out after slaughtering innocents. I had several of these cases, and one of them hit me particularly hard. It continues to haunt me.

The radio dispatcher sent us on a multiple-homicide call when I was a sergeant in that division. As directed, I drove to a dumpy old trailer park where everyone rented, nobody owned. It was three o'clock in the afternoon. Kids were everywhere, playing in tiny yards, standing by their bikes, their lives interrupted by a stream of ambulances, fire trucks, and police cars clogging the roads.

There was a uniform cop standing on the front porch of a sorry-looking house trailer that had probably outlived its warranty by twenty years. As I walked from my car toward the crime scene, the patrolman put his right hand down to his side and flashed three fingers.

Three bodies.

I nodded in acknowledgment as I pulled on my rubber gloves. I kept a box of five hundred in the car and usually started a week with fifty pairs in both pockets of my suit coats. I went through them fast.

The first victim was just inside the door, on the kitchen floor. An adult female propped in a sitting position against a cabinet. She was wearing shorts and a halter top. No shoes.

There were multiple gunshot wounds to her chest. Another in what had been her face. Her mouth was open. Her eyes were closed. Her hands were turned with her palms up, as if praying for divine intervention, or peace at last.

Next to her on the floor were several expended bullet casings from a semiautomatic pistol. These indicated that the shooter reloaded the gun. He could not confirm that, because he was dead and lying within six feet of her. He was approximately the same age, with an apparent self-inflicted gunshot wound to the head.

The gun was a few inches from his hand on the floor, where I would expect it to be in a murder-suicide scenario. Don't tell Hollywood, but after someone shoots himself, the muscles relax and the gun falls. It is rare to find the weapon still in hand.

The shooter–suicide victim's right temple had tattooing or stippling, which is burned flesh and bruising caused by muzzle flash and gunpowder from close-range gunshots and supersonic projectile entering flesh and bone.

Done with him, I looked around.

The patrol cop from the porch had come in and was standing behind me.

"You said three bodies."

"Back bedroom," he said.

His tone was particularly solemn and meant to prepare me for the worst, as if he could protect me from such evil. He didn't need to say any more, but he did, knowing that I had children.

"It's a kid."

I'd been a cop a long time by then. Still, my gut seized up.

"How old?" I asked.

"He's little."

Fuck.

I didn't want to go down that hallway, but I went.

He was no more than five years old, wearing his Mickey Mouse pajamas, clenching a stuffed animal to his chest. He had four close-range gunshot wounds to the head, which was grotesquely distorted. The explosion blew his left eye onto the mattress, which was soaked in blood. Flies buzzed around the bed.

How the fuck could anyone do this to a little kid? How could you do this to your child? What could a kid possibly say or do at age five to warrant such a violent death?

Nothing. Nothing at all.

His own father did that to him. We found the usual rambling suicide note on the kitchen table in cursive handwriting, left by our hero dead on the floor nearby. Can't go on. Life is so hard. Quotes from the Bible. He wanted to take them to heaven with him.

I've read so many of these. It was like the same guy wrote the same thing every time.

Still, this one will stay with me because of the boy in the bedroom. Day or night, it doesn't matter. I still see him on the blood-soaked mattress. I still smell the coppery scent of fresh blood.

My son had those exact same Mickey Mouse pajamas. He wore them out because he loved them so much.

Kids always got to me more than any other victims. They always seemed to be around the same age as my kids. Their rooms had the same posters. Their closets had the same clothes. They wore the same sneakers, had the same paperbacks, tapes, or CDs.

My son and daughter will tell you today that I was a loving dad who hugged them a lot, often for what to them seemed like no reason. They also will tell you that I tended to be quiet—okay, gloomy, so they and their friends usually walked circles around me. They didn't want to cross me. I never hit them or took it out on them, but they knew the violence of my work and how it churned within me.

I handled it, or thought I did, but most of our television show viewers don't want to be witnesses to the worst of what I saw. They shouldn't be. It can twist you up to see what humans are capable of doing to each other and to themselves, and particularly to those who trust them and love them.

MANCHILD ABUSE

This applies to children who have grown physically, but not mentally. All too often I was called upon to deal with the aftermath of parents ill-equipped to handle mentally disabled adult children.

I suppose his mother thought she was doing the right thing when she sent her forty-year-old, six-foot-eight, 300-pound mentally challenged son out into the neighborhood to find work. He'd never been violent. He was, in fact, known to be a gentle giant, who had done odd jobs for neighbors in the past. If a tree went down, he could pick it up, with one hand.

The son found more steady work after he was hired by a landscaper who'd relocated in their neighborhood. The owner worked him like a dog for two weeks, ordering him to move heavy bags of fertilizer, landscaping blocks, and bricks. The big guy did not complain. He thrived on hard work, and he expected to get paid for it.

The landscaper had other ideas. When payday came, he told the gentle giant to get lost and refused to pay him. The poor guy went home to his mother and told her. She told him to go back and demand payment.

He walked back to the landscaping place. The owner was in his office, decorated in sports memorabilia from his favorite teams. Among the memorabilia on display was an aluminum baseball bat bearing the logo of a college team. When the owner again refused to pay up, the gentle giant lost it.

He grabbed the baseball bat and swung away, breaking every bone in the landscaper's body. The bad boss crawled to the porch, but no farther.

When I arrived, there was blood dripping from the ceiling where the force of the blows had splattered it. The floor was soaked in blood, as was the ground beneath it.

The landscaper's body resembled a duffle bag stuffed with broken flesh and bones. His head was no bigger than a crushed can. Brain material was all over the front door. Other employees identified him by his work boots; nothing else was recognizable. The coroner estimated more than two hundred blows were delivered.

The batter, a sweet, friendly child of a man who'd been pushed beyond capacity, remained at the scene, soaked in blood, and mumbling, "He wouldn't pay me."

Sometimes parents kill their children with abuse and neglect, sometimes merely with disapproval. I went looking for an eleven-year-old kid who'd gone missing along with his grandfather's .22 rifle. We found his body not far from the house, on an abandoned railroad track. He'd put the end of the rifle barrel in his mouth and then pulled the trigger with his toe.

We interviewed the family and found that he had been a bright kid, a gifted student, whose demanding and domineering father had gone ape-shit crazy on him because he'd come home with a single B on his report card. Every other grade was an A.

The father's response was "How could you do this to me?"

Your son made sure it never happened again, now didn't he? It was the last B the poor kid ever brought home.

Just as an aside to this case, we had a small group of volunteer police chaplains—Protestant ministers, priests, and rabbis—who often came with us when we had to give a death notice in such cases. Their job was to give comfort to the family. We called the chaplains "sky pilots."

A new volunteer, a Baptist minister, accompanied me when I went to notify the family of this young suicide victim. He didn't seem to understand the nature of his role. When I knocked on the door and delivered the worst possible news to the distraught parents, he stood beside me with a stupid, lame smile on his face. He never offered a word of condolence or comfort. Not a single prayer. He just stood there smiling like a moron.

The family looked at him, and then they looked at me like, "Who the fuck is this guy and why is he smiling as you break my heart?"

After I dropped Rev. Smiley off, the first thing I did was call the office and have him removed from the chaplain corps. He was not fit for the job.

The oddly grinning Baptist wasn't the only sky pilot I grounded. On another case, I had to deliver the death notice of a Hispanic girl who'd been murdered by a guy she'd spurned in a bar. I knew her family was deeply involved in the Catholic Church. During the investigation, I'd seen pictures of the Virgin Mary all over the house.

We found the girl's body and I had to go tell the parents. It was around midnight, but this wasn't the sort of thing that could wait until morning. I called our contact number for the Catholic diocese in Colorado Springs, looking for a priest to accompany me so he could console this deeply religious family.

The priest who answered the phone at the diocese residence said, "We don't go out at night." That was it. His team kept banker's hours.

I hung up on the soulless priest and called a good-guy rabbi I'd known for years. I told him that the daughter of a Catholic family had been murdered but I couldn't get a priest to go with me for the notification.

"Why not?" the rabbi asked.

"Apparently, they don't go out at night."

"Bastards," he said.

I had no interest in igniting a holy war, or an unholy war, I just needed someone from the God Squad to be there when I delivered horrible news to these nice people.

"Come pick me up, I'll wing it," he said.

The rabbi wore a yarmulke skullcap but delivered a full round on the rosary in perfect Catholic. He stepped up and had the entire family on their knees praying in front of a Madonna statue in the living room.

On the ride home, I told my Jewish friend how impressed I was with his priest impersonation.

The rabbi replied: "I keep up with the competition."

COP HUMOR

I veered a little off topic with those two stories, but I figured you needed a break from my nightmare tales. Then again, it is true that another thing you never see on my television show is my smile. You may think that is part of my *Homicide Hunter* shtick, and to some degree that is true. It's not a cop comedy in the *Barney Miller* vein, or even *Brooklyn Nine-Nine*. We aren't trying to make our viewers laugh. It's a reality show and the reality is that my career as a homicide detective was a grim march from one murder investigation to another.

My career wasn't exactly a barrel of laughs. Kathy and the kids will tell you I wasn't all smiles at home, either. Yet, contrary to some reports, I do have a sense of humor, twisted as it may be. As anybody in law enforcement will tell you, we have our own brand of humor, which is purely a defense mechanism against all of the darkness we encounter. We either laugh or we cry.

My brand of cop humor would not translate well to my television show, but I will share some examples in this book. I am serious when I say my options were laughter or tears, because I dealt with so many cases that were just as bizarre as they were tragic and horrifying.

Case in point: I once walked into a murder scene and discovered a headless female body on the floor. The head was nowhere in sight. Before we could start searching, one of my guys said, "What do you think the cause of death was?"

Both bizarre and horrifying, right? Do you laugh or do you cry? My response: "I'm not a doctor, but I think she lost her head."

I didn't say cop humor was *good* humor.

We really didn't know how she'd died at that point even though we already had her husband locked up for her murder. He'd admitted to killing her during a psychotic episode of some sort. He was out of his mind, talking about the Bible, calling himself a demon named "Legion," muttering about a brood of vipers.

The case was basically solved, a ground ball to the shortstop, no big deal. Except that we had an incomplete corpse, which most judges consider bad form if you are going for a murder conviction.

The nutcase husband claimed he didn't remember a thing, even though he was covered in blood. We knew he hadn't left the house, so we began searching for his wife's missing part. Imagine looking for a severed head under the sofa, beneath the sofa cushions, in the bedroom, all the closets, and cabinets. Bedrooms, bathrooms, basement, living room, dining room . . . kitchen.

Not the kitchen, right? For lack of a better idea, I opened the refrigerator. Nothing unusual popped out at me, until I looked at the bottom crisper drawer. Normally this is where you store produce like apples, peaches, cantaloupes, honeydew, watermelons, and lettuce.

Or your murdered wife's head, if you happen to be a psychotic homicidal husband. I have to admit, she was well preserved, all things considered. In fact, her eyes and mouth were still open.

"Why would he put her head in there?" asked one of my fellow sleuths.

"I dunno, maybe he was hoping to make his wife a salad?"

DEATH IS NO PICNIC

Television is a visual medium. The producers of my show think in terms of scenes that will keep viewers engaged and entertained. It's a reality television show, but sometimes reality is just so grotesque there is no way to make it presentable for our audiences. It's no picnic, especially when the picnic is dripping in blood.

Normally, the Garden of the Gods park, located outside Colorado Springs, would provide a wonderful location for a television shoot. It's a beautiful place offering majestic views of towering red rock formations and Pikes Peak. Entry to the 1,300-acre park is free, but there is one picnic table in a canyon, a particularly scenic area of the park, that is so popular with visitors you have to make a reservation for it, often months in advance.

Our case began when a family's reserved time finally came. They went to that coveted spot to enjoy a meal with breathtaking views. They were having a great time, basking in natural splendor, until they saw a towering pine tree with its branches dripping blood all over the ground.

Further examination revealed a headless body hanging upside down near the top of the seventy-foot-tall tree, like a macabre Christmas ornament. The body had bled out, all eight or nine pints of blood, dripping through the pine branches.

Needless to say, the picnic was over. We were called to the scene. It took us a while to figure out what had happened, and even longer to retrieve the body from the treetop. This was not a murder. It was a suicide, a surprisingly popular pastime in beautiful Colorado. The last time I looked, Colorado ranked sixth among all U.S. states. Nobody knows why the rate is so high. I often dealt with three or four a month. My record was four in one day.

Homicide gets the call anytime a death occurs outside the medical environment. We have to determine method and manner. This was definitely not the usual overdose, hanging, or gassing. The guy climbed onto a cliff that stood above the pine tree, then blew his head off with a .41 Magnum round from a handgun. Next, the laws of physics kicked in.

His body fell forward, off the cliff and into the pine tree, where it lodged in the upper boughs and proceeded to drain on the picnic. We went up to the cliff to see what we could see. Winged and clawed members of nature's own cleanup crew were hard at work. A magpie was nibbling brain matter out of a piece of skullcap.

Retrieving the body from the tree posed challenges. It seems you can't cut a pine tree down in a designated national natural landmark without an act of Congress. We didn't have time for that, so we brought in a crane from the fire department. The crane operator apparently had a weak stomach because he took one look at the body in the tree, puked, and passed out.

I decided to do it myself. I climbed into the crane cab and figured out the mechanics of it and within a short time, we had the body out of the branches, in a bag, and headed for the morgue.

When I went home that night, Kathy bravely said, "How was your day?"

"It was interesting. I learned a new skill," I replied. "You ever need a dead guy plucked out of a tree, I'm your man."

PART II

MOTIVES FOR MURDER

FOUR

NICKEL-AND-DIMED
TO DEATH

I was never surprised at the motives for murders I investigated. Disappointed maybe, but not surprised. The primary motives for murder revolve around the unholy trio of money, sex, and revenge. Then there is the wild-card motive, depravity, which is the realm of drug-crazed maniacs, psychopaths, sociopaths, and serial killers. You wouldn't know it from all the book, television series, and movie plotlines they inspire but they are rare animals; deadly, but rare in the real world of crime.

I've often said that murder is simple, and that is true enough, but a killer may be driven by just one of these factors or any combination of them. Countless other motivations and personal triggers also come into play, including something that has recently become a major issue in politics—fake news.

You might be inclined to think fake news isn't a serious issue. I beg to differ. False information can lead to real bloodshed and great tragedy, as in the case of a murder I investigated in Colorado Springs. One day, a customer walked into a bank branch wanting to know his checking account balance. He was stressed out because of a long-running issue with his live-in girlfriend. She liked to buy things and she had champagne taste. He had a beer budget.

The bank customer suspected that despite his repeated demands, his girlfriend had bought another big-ticket item. He asked a teller for his checking balance.

The teller, who considered herself a bit of a comedian, did not know this guy, but she decided it was all right to yank his chain. Unfortunately, his chain was ready to snap.

The teller wisecracked something like: "Oh, your girlfriend was in here this morning and took all the money out."

It was not true, and it was the worst possible thing she could have said to that particular guy at that point in time. Before the teller could say, "Just kidding," the customer rushed out the door in a rage.

He found his girlfriend, and killed her.

The motive here? Out of the big three, money is most likely. It was the central issue in their long-running conflict. You could argue that even without the teller's comment, this guy was on track to kill the girlfriend anyway. Her shopping addiction was the real trigger. If the teller hadn't unknowingly lit his fuse, the next big purchase might have done the trick.

He was already on the edge, thinking: "If she goes shopping one more time, I'll kill her!" Over time, he developed the motive that made sense to him.

PRIMED FOR THE KILL

Most victims are killed by someone they know: a spouse, a lover, a coworker, a boss, their drug dealer or their drug customer. Emotions overcome judgement and to hell with the consequences.

Motive matters, but it should never be allowed to guide an investigation. So many killings make no sense at all if motive is the only consideration. Popeyes chicken wings may be one man's soul food and another man's junk food, but you wouldn't think to kill for it, or would you?

A thirty-six-year-old career criminal was paroled and released from prison to the custody of his eighty-year-old grandparents, a situation ripe for disaster. The dirtbag moved out of the joint and into grandma's house. One night his grandpa had a hankering for Popeyes' wings special while watching TV around 10 p.m. He went out and came back with a heaping box of wings.

The lowlife grandson wanted grandpa's wings all for himself. Grandpa had a problem with that. His loving grandson said, "Fuck you, Grandpa!" He grabbed the wings and devoured the entire box of greasy goodness.

Distraught, grandpa went to his bedroom and retrieved his .38 snub-nosed two-inch revolver. He then put six bullets in the grandson's grease-smeared face. When your trusty homicide detective arrived, there was still a partially eaten Popeyes wing in the hand of the deceased. Grandma was present, but too drunk to serve as a credible witness.

This senseless crime inspired me to briefly try a new career path. I suggested to fellow officers that we create an advertising slogan for Popeyes, featuring billboard portraits of this grandpa with his .38 standing over his grandson/victim with the caption: "I'd kill for a piece of Popeyes." An alternative billboard might have featured a bubble caption coming from the dead grandson saying, "I would die for a piece of Popeyes."

Madison Avenue did not jump all over my suggested campaign, so I remained in law enforcement. I did, however, incorporate this case in my training classes for new detectives. I used it to make the point that while murder motives are always interesting, you can't get hung up on them when beginning an investigation. The risk is that you make a presumption based on preliminary observations and then find yourself trying to prove it, rather than letting the evidence and the facts guide your investigation.

When I taught at the police academy, I would show the classes a photograph of a pretty blond woman who'd been shot and killed. She had multiple gunshot wounds at slightly different angles. She was lying in a pool of blood. This was a color photograph and very graphic. I could always hear the cadets suck wind when I projected the photo on the screen.

Then I would ask them, "When you arrive at this murder scene, should you sit there and agonize about the motive; why this happened?"

Inevitably a cadet would raise his hand and say, "Isn't that what we are supposed to do?"

My answer was, "Not really."

Why a murder happened is not nearly as important to investigating a crime as the question of what happened. Establishing the "what" leads to the why. The facts of the case lead you to the motive. The key is to focus on the facts first. Instead of speculating that the woman was shot because her husband was tired of her buttering the toast on the wrong side, you need to study what you are looking at, because the facts might lead you to an entirely different motive. Maybe she was shot by a serial murderer who thinks all pretty blondes are she-devils and it is his God-given role to eliminate them from the earth.

Hey, I've had crazier cases.

Rather than trying to determine a motive at that point, I tell the class to study the crime scene with an open mind and let the facts lead them to the motive. My advice is to take those facts and work on *what* happened before worrying about *why* it happened and making assumptions that could lead you astray.

I will walk you through the crime scene in the photo in more detail in the chapter on investigating crime scenes. For now, I'll just say that the photo of the crime scene provides a shitload of information that will be helpful in the investigation. Let's look at the three most common motives for murder—money, sex, and revenge—and then at the wild-card fourth reason, pure depravity.

THE ROOT OF ALL EVIL

A Bible passage (1 Timothy 6:10) is often cited as the source of the phrase "Money is the root of all evil." The passage comes from Apostle Paul's first letter to a young disciple, Timothy. It goes like this, according to one translation: "For the love of money is a root of all kinds of evil. Some people, eager for money, have wandered from the faith and pierced themselves with many griefs."

So, it's the *love* of money, not money itself, that is the root of all evil, according to Paul. I have to agree. In fact, the same holds true with all three of the primary motives for murder on my list. What drives people to kill isn't money, sex, or revenge; it is the emotions attached to each of them that leads to so many killings.

There is nothing inherently evil about money or sex or revenge, after all. Money can help you feed, clothe, and raise your loved ones. Or you can give it away and make a lot of other people very happy. Sex is also considered a good thing by many people, or so I'm told. Some of my closest friends enjoy sex. You and I wouldn't be here if it weren't for sex. Now, the beneficial aspects of revenge may not be quite so obvious, but it can be a great motivator: *You beat me in the championship game last year so this year I'm going to work harder so I can beat you and win it all!*

Once again, the emotions we attach to these factors are what cloud our judgment and drive us to do irrational things like murder. This is especially true with money, because, in my experience, most murders are committed over relatively small amounts of it. Maybe not in the movies or on television, but in real life, murder is a small-change transaction fueled by huge amounts of rage.

Money is the most common motive for murder on the street. Drugs and money are a particularly lethal combination for the young and feckless. Toss in a little Ivory soap and you have a clean case for a homicide, one that I solved involving a nineteen-year-old entrepreneur who decided that selling crack was too dangerous.

He sold fake crack instead. Street name: "bunk junk."

Thinking himself clever, he bought bars of Ivory soap and whittled them into small waxy, white chips resembling crack cocaine. These days you can buy a pack of ten bars for between three or four dollars. It was even cheaper back then. The kid was selling each soap chip for twenty dollars, so his profit margin probably seemed like a huge boon in his addled mind.

Unfortunately for his life span, the numb-nuts fake drug dealer did not think much beyond the initial point of purchase, the front seat of his car. His customers were not Mensa members, but the drug zombies still recognized they'd been scammed when soap bubbles rose from their crack pipes. Some might have noted the clean, fresh Ivory scent, but crackheads typically don't have the greatest senses of smell due to ravaged nasal cavities.

Another problem with the kid's target market: Crackheads are more inclined to express their outrage with violence than say, filing a complaint with the Better Business Bureau. They are paranoid, armed to the teeth, fucked up, and ready to fuck up others at all times.

No surprise then, when one of them returned to the kid's car, caught him with his Ivory crack, and shot him between the eyes. This murder motive was obvious: a money-revenge combo. The real challenge was determining which of the kid's many soaped-up customers pulled the trigger. An added impediment: The drug world is not a detective-friendly environment. No one knows nothin'. Crackheads don't know each other's real names and addresses. They are often too whacked out to be aware of anything occurring around them, or even *to* them.

For all of the above reasons, we worked the Ivory dope case for four months before we nailed the shooter, who was out only twenty bucks for the crack but would lose more than twenty years of his freedom for the murder. It makes no sense. Homicide motives are often like that. I had another case where a customer owed his drug dealer all of fifteen dollars. The dealer didn't really need the money, but he decided to make an example out of the guy so other customers didn't think they could cheat him.

He tracked down the guy, killed him, and took fifteen dollars out of the wad of cash in the dead guy's jeans. He then put the rest of the cash back in his pocket because, after all, his victim only owed him fifteen bucks. This brings to mind a bit of advice I often share: To avoid becoming a murder victim, stay away from illegal drugs, drug dealers, drug users, drug dens, and drug lords. This has been a public service announcement.

SMALL CHANGE, BIG CRIMES

Taverns, especially those with pool tables, and motorcycle gangs hanging out, are another good place to avoid if you prefer a natural death after a long life instead of being shot, stabbed, or beaten to death with a cue stick or an eight ball. Fifty cents can get you killed in a place like that.

Two coworkers were in a bar in Colorado Springs, drinking and playing pool. Shooting eight ball. The loser of each game was supposed to pay for the next round. Two quarters in the slot. Push it in. The balls drop. Game on.

Simple enough. Then again, alcohol complicates the simplest of things. One guy lost count of the score. He couldn't remember who won and who lost. He insisted that his opponent pay up. The other guy said it was his coworker's turn. The argument went ballistic. One pulled out a .45 automatic and blasted the other in the chest. The victim was dead before he hit the green felt.

Murdered for fifty cents. Rack 'em up.

Pool money, gas money, drug money—the murders I dealt with were mostly small change. The highest dollar amount I can ever remember as a motive in one of my murder cases was $200,000, but that wasn't cash in hand, exactly. A guy decided to dump his wife, but just divorcing her apparently wasn't an option. He figured he needed a bundle of money to start his new life with his new wife, or girlfriend.

This mope was not particularly creative. You've heard the plot a million times. He decided to kill his wife and cash in on her death so that he and his girlfriend could live happily ever after. He took out a $100,000 insurance policy on his wife without telling her. It had a double indemnity clause that paid $200,000 if the wife was murdered.

My, my, my. Did he not think the insurance policy on his wife might set off red flags and flashing sirens if she happened to suffer a violent death? Maybe it did, but greed and desperation trumped all.

If you think he was a dunce, meet his doofus girlfriend. She let Romeo convince her to kill his wife for him. Granted, it took him eight months to talk her into a capital offense, but he did it. They concocted a hare-brained plan straight out of *Law and Order for Dummies*. She pretended to be an armed robber and shot the wife on a busy street.

Brilliant! This motive was clearly money, but the contributing factor here was blatant stupidity. You might be surprised to learn that the husband and his girlfriend were both college graduates. She had two kids. He had three. If nothing else, they should have realized that $200,000 wouldn't exactly put them on easy street for the rest of their lives.

As I noted, that is the highest dollar amount that ever served as a murder motive in cases that came my way. There was one with higher stakes, but it wasn't money found, it was money lost.

Two business partners had a project that they thought would net them $500,000 to a million dollars. When the deal blew up, Partner X blamed Partner Y, saying he'd cost him hundreds of thousands, at least.

I came to see this as a case of Dumb versus Dumber. Partner X claimed Partner Y was a moron for blowing the deal. Maybe he was right. Then again, Partner X decided his next best move should be to go to a strip club, yes, a strip club, and ask his favorite strippers if they knew a hit man for hire.

Of course, they did. They were strippers. They told Partner X the hit man would do it for $10,000. The stripper and the hit man screwed up and got themselves arrested. They couldn't wait to tell our officers the names of those who put them up to the botched murder-for-hire scheme. I went to the office of Partner X and announced that he was under arrest. He went down like a sack of shit, collapsed on his desk.

I thought he'd had a heart attack and died, but he'd just passed out from an overdose of idiocy. Partner X went to prison. Partner Y lived to make more deals, probably bad ones.

FIVE

KILLER SEX

S ex can lead to death in many strange and sordid ways. It can be a motive for murder, or a factor that leads to death. Guys may joke about wanting to die while having sex in their old age, but that's a little tough on the other person involved—if there is another person involved.

The murders that I handled in which sex was a motive were almost always the result of Partner A cheating on Partner B with Partner C. Sometimes there was a D, E, and F hanging around, too. If a husband catches his wife cheating, the typical response for the man is to kill everyone in the room, namely the wife and her lover, too. But if the wife catches a husband cheating, she'll often spare the lover and just kill the philandering spouse. Women are just more forgiving, I guess.

Still, a woman scorned can be lethal. I often use the following sex motive case to explain the difference between first- and second-degree murder. In Colorado, if the victim engages in a highly provoking act that causes an irresistible rise of passion in the perpetrator, and there is insufficient time for a voice of reason to be heard before death results, it is a crime of passion and therefore second-degree murder. To make the cut for first-degree murder, you must demonstrate malice aforethought. This means the killer has taken time to plan and plot the murder.

My favorite example of this is a young wife who found out that her young husband was having an affair with a young coworker. The wife did her own surveillance to confirm her suspicions. She saw her husband and his lover kissing in the office parking lot.

She didn't confront her cheatin' man. Instead she waited for an opportunity to catch him in flagrante delicto. A few months after the parking lot incident, the husband announced that he had to leave town for a business meeting. When he pulled out of the driveway, she gave him a ten-count and followed.

He went to a motel, where his paramour met him. The stalker wife gave them just enough time to get under the covers before she went into the hotel office and convinced the manager to give her a key to the room. She told the manager that she wanted to play a practical joke on a coworker who had rented the room. The manager reported later that she was a very convincing and funny actress. She had him in stitches.

The husband wasn't so lucky.

His spouse's mood had darkened by the time she came through the door swinging an aluminum baseball bat. She caught the object of her disaffection in a highly vulnerable position. He screamed at the first few blows, but his raging wife swung for the fences, fracturing his skull.

The naked and cowering coworker stayed under the covers. She was spared. We found her bloodied, shaking and shrieking beneath the sheets, but prepared to testify, once the wife-gone-wild was locked up.

At the scene of the crime, she expressed shock that we even took her into custody. The not-grieving widow said he deserved it. We reminded her that a better play would have been to hire a divorce lawyer, take half of her ex-husband's money, and move on to a new life. Instead, she moved into a correctional facility.

She went down for first-degree murder because even if this was a crime of passion, she had planned and plotted her assault over several months. The only way her lawyers could have made a case for second-degree murder was if she were an avid baseball player who carried her aluminum bat at all times and just happened to walk in on the debauchery.

That was the scenario in another sex motive case. The husband was in the U.S. Army. He carried a .45 automatic pistol as his side-arm every day when he went to work at Fort Carson. He worked the midnight shift. He left one night as usual to go to work. Halfway to the base, he realized he forgot his ID card. He could not enter the base without it. He turned around and headed back home.

When he returned, he found a strange car in his driveway. He walked in the house and saw his wife at the top of the stairs, hastily drawing a bathrobe around her nakedness.

"What are you doing?" he asked.

She was nervous and unresponsive.

He was not an idiot.

The husband ran up the stairs past her, entered his bedroom, opened the closet door, and beheld a naked stranger.

The husband then drew his .45 automatic and lit up said naked stranger.

Seven rounds at close range did the job.

Lucky for the wife, he ran out of ammo.

The avenged husband put down the gun, sat at the top of the stairs, and waited for us to arrive. He confessed at the scene and later pleaded guilty.

It was a slam-dunk, classic case of second-degree murder. A crime of passion. There was a highly provoking act and insufficient time for the voice of reason to assert itself. The gun was there, as it always was. He was armed and overwhelmed with rage. Boom. Boom. Boom.

As a side note: Don't ever hide in the closet. They always look in the closet.

MESSAGE IN A BOTTLE

Our strongest instinct is survival. When our lives are threatened, that instinct triggers the fight-or-flight response. Next up on the powerful-instinct list is sex, which can trigger cheating on a spouse or partner. Infidelity has only a few variations, but the methods for responding to it seem infinite.

Even a run-of-the-mill cheating spouse case can surprise you. They often surprised me. A guy came home and found his wife in bed naked with her equally naked boyfriend. The boyfriend dove out a second-floor window and hit the ground running through the neighborhood.

He got away. The wife wasn't so fleet of foot.

The husband just happened to be an avid collector of vintage soda bottles. In the history of the Coke and Pepsi cola wars, there was a time in the 1950s and '60s when the rival companies developed bottles of heavy glass that could withstand harsh handling by distributors and vending machines. Coke had bulletproof bottles in a light green tint. Pepsi had clear bottles that incorporated a spiral design. Both were quite heavy. Both became collector's items.

This husband had 150 of them in a display case. After finding his wife and her boyfriend between the sheets, he grabbed a heavy glass Pepsi bottle from his collection and beat the wife to death with it. The coroner estimated that he hit her more than one hundred times. You could pretty much tally them by the tracks of blood on the ceiling.

Her head was a half-inch high and flat, unrecognizable as a human from the neck up. The bottle did not break.

I found the husband sitting on the sofa. He'd already been cuffed. Blood dripped from his face and hair. He looked at me with eyes the size of silver dollars. He appeared to be in a zombie trance. He had no clue of the horrors he'd wrought in his psychotic rage.

"Is she gonna be all right?" he asked.

I considered telling him things might have gone better with a Coke, but I let it go.

SEXUAL PREDATORS AND THEIR PREY

Infidelity isn't the only scenario in which sex can be a motive for murder and mayhem, of course. Sexual predators have been known to kill their innocent victims, although sometimes the tables get turned and the bad guy gets a bullet. As you might suspect, I love it when *that* happens. Fort Carson in Colorado Springs is home to approximately 25,000 people, including members of the Fourth Infantry Division and the Tenth Special Forces Group. There are many young married couples living on and around the base, as you might expect.

You could reasonably expect also that these young couples with military ties are among the most well armed in the greater Colorado Springs area. Even the stay-at-home military moms. Yet that thought either did not matter or did not occur to a sexual predator and burglar who broke into the condo townhouse of a twenty-year-old soldier, his nineteen-year-old wife, and their infant.

The young mother and baby were home alone because her husband was "downrange," which means that he was on a thirty-day field exercise way out in the far reaches of the 137,000-acre military base. The sexual predator and burglar was not subtle in his break-in. He kicked in the front door, which awakened the mother.

Her bedroom was upstairs, which gave her enough time to grab her child and the .22 Magnum revolver her husband had provided. She'd had some training from her husband in how to respond to such a threat. She didn't have a high level of skill, just enough.

She went to the top of the staircase to confront the intruder, who was wearing dark clothing. He laughed when he saw the young mother holding her baby in one arm and aiming the pistol at him because her hand was shaking badly.

"Get out of my house," she said

He laughed again and came up the staircase.

He was halfway up when she turned her face away and pulled the trigger. She put one round through his aorta and dropped him. He was dead before he hit the bottom step.

The intruder had an extensive record for burglary and sexual assault. He'd just been released from prison.

I found him fish-eyed and unresponsive. The mother was a mess. Her baby was crying. She was crying.

"Am I going to jail?" she asked in quivering tones.

"No, my dear," I said. "You did a good thing. It was clearly self-defense. I will have this dead piece of shit removed from your house so you and your baby can go back to bed."

She seemed relieved, but then a guilty look came over her face.

"I turned away when I pulled the trigger," she said.

"Well, you got him anyway, and that is what you needed to do because he was a dangerous and evil man."

It was poetic in my view. Finally, someone who could have been a victim stepped on this snake's neck instead. Had she not shot him when she did, it could have gone bad in a hurry. She could have missed him, but she didn't. She had every reason to believe he was intent on causing her serious bodily harm. The law says she was justified in using deadly force because he was coming at her.

Those circumstances make all the difference. If you are in

bed on the ground floor and some guy you don't know is coming through your window, you should say, "Get out of my house," and if the person keeps advancing in the dark toward you, then you are justified in lighting him up. That is self-defense.

However, if you say, "Get out of my house," and the intruder looks up and says, "Oh my God, wrong house," and begins to withdraw, then he is no longer a threat and if you shoot him in the back you could face a third-degree murder charge. If that person is fresh out of prison and has a prior record of burglaries leading to sexual assaults, the odds would tilt in your favor, however.

UNHAPPY ENDINGS

Another way that sex can, and does, lead to unhappy endings is known in cop lingo as "death by sexual misadventure." The motivation is to achieve sexual satisfaction through high-risk and dangerous practices, so, technically, I guess you can say sex is the motive in these cases. The most common of these are erotic asphyxiation and autoerotic asphyxiation.

These also are known as "edge games," because they take you to the edge of dying—when things go as planned.

When things don't go as planned, the coroner and law enforcement get the call. In a typical erotic asphyxiation, Partner A chokes Partner B during sex to deplete oxygen flow to the brain. This can enhance orgasm, and it also can lead to a terribly unhappy ending. If Partner A gets too aggressive in choking Partner B, the result is death for B and murder charges against A.

My position, and that of many prosecuting attorneys and jurors, is that if you are choking someone and they die, you killed them—even if you just wanted your friend to have fun. All too often, defense attorneys desperate for an angle will latch on to this as an alibi after a client has just flat out strangled someone. The infamous "Preppie Killer" case in New York's Central Park in the

1980s serves as a high-profile example of the jury *not* buying that defense. Good for them.

Autoerotic asphyxiation is even more common, in my experience. This occurs when someone concocts a way to deplete oxygen flow to their own brain while masturbating. This usually involves using a rope, belt, or even a dog choke collar that can be tightened to the point of orgasm and then released. Except, all too often, something goes awry and the edge gamer becomes a corpse.

I had to investigate several deaths like this during my career, both adults and juveniles. They are remarkably similar. We'd arrive and find the body along with pornographic magazines or photographs. The body would be hanging in a closet or from a doorknob or shower bar. Whatever device they'd created to reduce airflow to the brain failed to release as planned. In some cases, alcohol or drugs impaired the operator.

Usually a family member or loved one had found them and it was an awful situation, extremely distressing. Parents especially would try to cover up what happened by cutting the child down, dressing him, and cleaning up the scene. That always made it tougher because the last thing I wanted to do was threaten the grieving parents with arrest.

Most of them could not stick with their lies for long. They'd crack when I told them, "Look, I don't believe it happened the way you are saying it happened, so just tell me the truth."

In other cases, the family would be so mortified and shocked, they would freeze, unable to do anything. They'd just call us. These were delicate situations. There is nothing worse than losing a child and these cases were always among the most horrifying, senseless, and cruel.

I had an especially troubling case with a sixteen-year-old boy who was an honor student and seemed to be everything a parent could want in a child. His parents came home from work and found the door to his bedroom locked. They called his name and received no response.

Once they were able to get inside, they discovered him in the closet, nude, dead, and hanging by the neck from the garment bar. There were standard porn magazines in front of him, nothing exotic, just *Playboy* and *Hustler*.

The parents weren't aware of this sort of thing. They initially thought it was a suicide. They didn't touch him or go near the evidence. They called 911. They were so distraught they couldn't talk when I arrived. I went to his room. He had rigged a device to restrict the airflow to his brain while he masturbated. He was hanging with his toes barely off the ground. He had a knot to pull with his right hand to release it, but something had happened; the rope overlapped the knot so that when he pulled on it, the noose around his neck tightened instead. He died with the release cord in his hand.

No parent should see a child who dies in this way. Because the ligature injuries restrict blood supply, the face turns purple, enlarged and distorted, all but unrecognizable. We photographed the body and the closet, took measurements for our report, and took him down off the bar. We had to preserve the bar and the knot as evidence for the coroner, so they were placed on the gurney with the body.

The parents watched as his body was removed on the gurney with the bar and knot beside him. They screamed in anguish as we tried to get him out of there. The rod kept whacking the bannister on the way down. It was a horrific scene. Something you never recover from.

Mothers and fathers never expect to bury a child. There is no greater pain. This was a family with a nice home in an upper-middle-class neighborhood. They had other kids. Their son was on the lacrosse team, president of the debate club, and the top student in his class; the leading candidate to be valedictorian. Everyone loved him.

No one wanted to believe that he had died like he did. The official manner of death in these cases is given as "accidental" and the cause of death is "strangulation." I didn't take it beyond that, but it's usually the case that that vague description isn't enough for the media or curious neighbors and friends.

The news media sticks with the official manner and cause of death in their reporting, but editors and reporters talk to their friends, or they feel the need to explain the circumstances to outraged callers demanding to know the truth. Or someone knows someone who was at the scene, like an EMT; or a member of the coroner's staff leaks the report, and eventually the details come out. Then people get outraged and say it can't be true.

In this case, we were accused of covering up something. It's easier for some to say the police are lying than it is to accept the truth. Animosity is generated. They hate you and they don't mind telling you. There is no point defending yourself or getting in a pissing contest with grieving friends and family. They will torture you to cover their grief.

I understood their pain and their outrage. I learned to take the verbal abuse and move on. I could not help them recover. They were too emotional to respond to reason or accept the truth. They lost a child, the worst of all things, in a horrifying and senseless manner.

This family thought we destroyed their son's reputation, even though we did not talk to anyone about our findings. We did what we were supposed to do. We have to determine what happened and we can't lie on our reports for the sake of being nice. I don't do nice. I do death.

In my line of work, people either hate you or fear you or they both hate and fear you. If they are parents of the suspect, they hate you because they think you charged the wrong guy. If they are parents of the victim, they hate you because you didn't shoot the killer when you had the chance. There are no wins. Nobody wants to deal with the facts. They would rather drive themselves into hatred because it is easier to hate than to consider the truth.

Over the years, I had every kind of grief response imaginable, and some that I'd never dreamed possible. Late in my career, I took a young detective named Steve with me to notify a family that a teen boy had been murdered. I wanted this younger detective to learn about the best methods for doing a death notification as humanely as possible.

We knocked on the door and a smiling teenage girl answered. I showed my badge and asked if her parents were home.

"Oh, sure, Officers, please come in," she said.

She was so nice, it nearly broke my heart. I thought: *If you knew why we are here, you would not invite us in.*

The mother then appeared. She was a large woman, with a man's broad shoulders. She wasn't overweight. She was tall, thick, and strong. Her husband walked up behind her and stayed there, obviously wary and fearful.

I had learned to deliver tragic news in a straightforward manner, but without being overly specific, and that is what I did.

"I'm sorry to say that your son is no longer alive," I said.

The mother had a powerful and unexpected grief response. She grabbed Steve's tie and collapsed to the floor, yanking him down on top of her. This set off the family dog to barking so loud it made my ears ring.

I dropped to the floor and tried to break the mother's grip on Steve's tie because he was gasping for air. She then latched on to me, squeezing me in her arms. I finally got loose from her death grip and her husband pulled her away from us.

I offered our condolences and headed out the door, saying we'd be in touch when we had more information. On our way to the car,

I told Steve that this was not a normal scenario for a death notification. He looked at me with utter disbelief.

In truth, there really is no "normal" grief response in these situations. Some family members break down sobbing and others break out laughing. I've also seen a few turn to stone.

I had a case in which the victim's family was in rural Oklahoma, so a sheriff's deputy in their area did the death notification for me. When he explained that the son had died in my jurisdiction and that I'd handled the case, the father asked the deputy to call me so he could talk to me.

The deputy called. I answered and, after he explained what was going on, he put the father on the line. I was expecting him to be tearful, but he was ice cold.

"So, you got my kid up there in Colorado?" he asked.

I said yes.

"Can I bury him in Oklahoma?" he asked.

I told him to contact a local funeral home and they'd arrange to transport the body home for him.

"Would I have to pay for that?" he asked.

"Yes, you probably would," I said.

"Well then, you can keep him," said the father.

They were not close, obviously.

His cold-blooded response contrasted with most I witnessed. Sometimes grieving parents and family members would stay in touch for years after the case was closed. Others remembered me, long after I'd forgotten them.

One day I made a rare trip to the mall with my wife Kathy and our then-teenage daughter Kristin. Suddenly, a woman came out of nowhere calling my name, crying and carrying on.

I moved in front of Kristin, unsure of the woman's agenda.

"Detective Kenda, you were so good to me when our daughter was murdered," she said through her tears.

Just then her husband walked up, and he was teared up, too.

The mother then wrapped her arms around me and we stood there awkwardly for several seconds. Finally, I gently broke her grip, stepped back, and said, "Thank you, and, again, I'm sorry for your loss."

As we walked away, Kristin said, "Who was that?"

I replied: "I'm embarrassed to report that I have no idea."

I had far too many murdered daughters and too many grieving mothers in my life. I couldn't keep them all in my head. Not if I wanted to be a functioning human being.

TANGLED WEBS WEAVED

Cases involving sex always seemed to be more emotional for all parties involved, probably because of their lurid nature and the public embarrassment that can result. The individuals involved often came up with twisted fictional stories to avoid admitting the truth. It is human nature, and like most cops, I heard some doozies concocted to explain bizarre sexual behaviors.

In one particularly strange case, the ER administrator from a hospital called our radio dispatcher to report an assault victim who was at death's door due to extreme blood loss. They managed to pump enough blood into him to keep him alive until I got there. The ER doctor could only shake his head at this one. They saw as much weirdness as we did, but this was a new twist, or grind.

As he explained the patient's injuries, I understood the doctor's shock. The guy's penis and scrotum appeared to have been run through a shredder. Those vital parts were gone. All that remained was a bloody mess. The victim had lost 80 percent of his blood.

At that point, all we knew was that he'd driven himself to the hospital and collapsed on the driveway, where an employee found him. The doctor thought they could save him, but advised me to come back in three days or so because the guy was going to be out of it at least that long.

The guy made it, but he probably wished he hadn't.

The three-day interlude allowed the patient time to concoct quite a story. By his account, he was home in his apartment, innocently watching television (probably PBS) and minding his own business, when three black males in ski masks crashed through the door. They were heavily armed, of course. They set about stealing all of his earthly goods. Then they held him down and eviscerated his penis and scrotum while taunting him. By his account, they said white guys should not be allowed to have sex.

Quite a story, don't you agree? I've heard a lot of them and if this wasn't the worst it was certainly in the top five. I made it clear that my bullshit detector was registering in the red zone, and I invited him to try again with a somewhat more believable tale.

He went wide-eyed, turned scarlet, and stammered wildly. This set off alarms on the machines monitoring his vital signs. Rather than kill him, I decided to give him time to be more, or less, creative. He wasn't going anywhere for a while anyway.

"Just think about this for a while," I said. "In the meantime, I will obtain a search warrant and we will check out your apartment to see if conditions there confirm your story."

We did as promised; we waltzed into his apartment manager's office with a search warrant. He took us to the victim's place. No surprise, the door was not torn off its hinges. It was intact and unmolested. We entered with a key in the lock.

Nothing within the apartment appeared to be disturbed. Nothing was thrown on the floor. The television and stereo were in place.

There was blood—quite a bit of it—on the living room floor. It was confined to that area. The only other strange thing: Sitting in the blood zone was a Hoover canister vacuum.

I turned to my fellow detective and said, "If I open that canister, what do you suppose I will find inside?"

"A cock and a pair of balls?" he mused.

Dr. Watson was never so on target. We both deduced, correctly as it turned out, that our horribly mangled friend had nearly Hoovered himself to death by sticking his penis too far inside the machine where the impeller blades did their designated job, seizing what came their way.

We returned to the hospital with our findings. Within a few seconds, the patient confirmed that his initial story was pure fantasy. He admitted that he'd used the vacuum to pleasure himself sexually a number of times, but in this instance, he and his penis went a little too far. *His testicles were collateral damage.*

We didn't charge him with anything. He'd suffered enough for his sins. He also was responsible for a slew of Hoover jokes around the police department over several months.

To give women equal time, they too have their share of strange sexual misadventures. Another ER room call led me to a female patient, a twenty-eight-year-old single, professional woman. She'd come into the hospital after midnight with a railroad spike stuck through the palm of her right hand. She'd collapsed in the admitting area with a bloody rag wrapped around the hand.

I found her conscious and awaiting the arrival of a hand surgeon, who had his work cut out for him. The ER doctor said she was not on drugs or alcohol. When I inquired as to what happened, she drew a deep breath and exhaled quite a story.

She'd left her work place at 10 p.m. As she went to her car, six armed males confronted her in the parking lot. *Six armed males?*

My eyebrows raised to half-mast on the incredulity scale.

They shot up all the way when she said all six of her kidnappers piled into her Yugo with her in tow. Packing seven adults into a Yugo would likely take careful planning, not to mention hours of positioning and several bottles of baby oil. Crowbars or shoehorns might also be required.

Ah, but then her story turned even stranger still.

The kidnappers drove our alleged victim to Manitou Springs, which is just a few miles northwest of Colorado Springs. Just past Red Rock Canyon, it is home to ancient cliff dwellings as well as many grand old turn-of-the-century mansions that have been converted into B&B's or museums.

The mountain town is also host to many wild tales of resident ghouls, devil worshippers, and haunted places. Among them is a 1920s-era hotel that resembles a castle. It's on a hill in a residential area. Our alleged victim says her abductors took her to the grounds of the abandoned castle hotel. There, for reasons known only to warlocks and witches, they nailed her to a tree with the railroad spike through her hand.

As the enchanted evening continued, they stripped her naked, rubbed vegetable oil on her, and danced around her in the moonlight. Or so she said.

According to her vibrant tale, the devil worshippers became so caught up in their frenzied dancing that they didn't notice their captive yanking her spiked hand from the tree and fleeing with the spike still embedded in her palm. She feared if she removed it, she would bleed out.

Despite her spike, she then thumbed a ride to the hospital.

When she'd finished this grim fairy tale, my response was, "Do you really think I believe this bullshit? Please start over, with the truth this time."

While she obviously had mental issues, the young woman didn't have it in her to spin yet another fanciful yarn. She straight up admitted that she'd been drinking and somewhere in her twisted mind she decided it would be cool to masturbate with the railroad spike.

What she lacked in good sense, she made up for in sexual deviance. In her stupor, or whatever she was in, our spunky sybarite upped the ante by spiking herself through the hand. She thought it would boost her orgasmic delight.

I didn't need to know any more. I was afraid my brain would be permanently scarred. They aren't lying when they say truth is stranger than fiction, especially when it comes to sexual perversions. And it just kept getting stranger and stranger on my watch.

Another call: A young woman was found with her right arm repeatedly slashed and bleeding profusely on the quad of a small liberal arts college in the center of Colorado Springs. Campus security called 911 and took her to the emergency room, where she was treated and stabilized. It seems yet another masked man was on the loose. He materialized out of nowhere and confronted our victim, slashing at her arm repeatedly with an unknown sharp weapon. Masked Man then vaporized into thin air.

He did not try to rob her or sexually assault her. He just viciously sliced and diced her arm. She had no clue who did this horrible thing to her. Initially, neither did I.

The alarmed college administration put out a press release, fearing there was a slasher on the loose. The story hit the radio and television stations and the newspaper the next day. "Police baffled by violent assault on campus!"

Baffled! They loved it when we were baffled. While we were busy being baffled no children were safe and the mad slasher remained on the loose, lurking behind every bush, tree, and houseplant.

Everyone was up in arms. Students and their parents. The college president. The mayor and council. Every law-abiding citizen. A violent maniac was on the loose.

No pressure on me. None at all.

The only baffling thing was the girl's story. It made no sense. She had no defensive wounds like you'd typically expect on someone who'd fought off an attacker with a knife or other sharp weapon. No cuts to her hands, her other arm, legs, or face. Not even any bruises or red marks.

I interviewed her a couple of times at great length and decided she was garden-variety kooky, but not under the influence of alcohol or drugs. Finally, I told her that I didn't think anyone had attacked her.

"I'm pretty good at spotting bullshit and your story is bullshit," I said. "There was no him. There was just you."

She didn't respond well, so I decided to see what the evidence had to say. I told her I wanted to examine the clothing she'd been wearing when she came to the hospital.

"Why do you want to do that?"

"Evidence doesn't lie."

The ER team had cut off her clothing and bagged and stored it. There wasn't much to see. She hadn't been wearing a bra or panties, which isn't all that unusual for college girls. The bag contained only her long-sleeve shirt, jeans, and sneakers. The jeans and blouse were soaked in blood. The odd thing was that the right sleeve on her blouse was intact. No cuts or tears on the sleeve for the arm that had been cut to the bone repeatedly.

If a knife-wielding maniac assaults your arm, he doesn't let you roll up your sleeves first.

Things got more interesting when I searched the right rear pocket of her jeans. I found a razor blade covered in blood. There was a very nice fingerprint in the blood on the blade, which proved to be a match for the girl's left thumb.

I returned to the hospital, wading through the dogs of the press broadcasting on the hour with updates on the mad-slasher case.

I entered the room of the "victim" with the bloody blade in a paper bag.

"You know what this is, don't you?" I asked. "Is this what you used on your arm?"

She looked at the razor in the bag, then she stared at the floor.

The truth spilled out: She discovered, somehow, that she had more intense orgasms if she masturbated while looking at her own blood.

"They are very intense," she said.

I don't get creeped out easily. This came close.

She was in her dorm room on her bed, naked and cutting herself with the razor blade as she masturbated. She was having one orgasm after another and then suddenly realized she'd gone too far with the cutting. Feeling sick and faint, she was on the edge of passing out while bleeding from her self-inflicted wounds. She threw on a blouse and jeans and went looking for help. Had she remained in her dorm room, she likely would have bled to death.

She made only a couple of steps into the quad before collapsing. Lucky for her, a security guard was on patrol and came by shortly after she went down.

Good heavens! Who are these people and what planet are they from? It is beyond me how anyone would get off on seeing their own blood. Maybe I lack creativity.

All right then, enough about sex as a motive for madness. Let's move on to something homicidal, yet wholesome—good old-fashioned revenge!

SIX

A THIRST FOR VENGEANCE

There was a very successful street entrepreneur in my city who sold heroin. Let's call him Luther. He was very good at his job, bringing in about $200,000 a week.

Now, Luther had a rival heroin dealer whose market was in another part of the city. Let's call him Frankie. He and Luther didn't compete head-to-head, so they got along. In fact, when Frankie found himself running short on his product one day, he asked Luther to sell him some so he could keep his customers stoned until a new supply arrived.

Frankie promised to pay Luther, who sent over some heroin.

But then, come payday, Frankie refused, claiming it was "bad shit."

Luther had a thriving business. He did not need the money, but heroin is a tough market. A dealer who forgives debts will soon be buried in it. Luther knew that if he let Frankie slide on this payment, word would get out and soon others would be screwing with him.

On a visit to family members in Kansas, Luther met some bad guys at a party. He recruited them to come to Colorado Springs and kill Frankie. He provided specific instructions, telling them to shoot Frankie in the face after first delivering a message. They were to tell Frankie that Luther was collecting on his debt, with interest.

The Kansas killers fulfilled their assignment. They tracked down Frankie and shot him eight times in the face at close range. Debt paid. Revenge exacted.

My homicide detective team compiled a list of Frankie's enemies and potential killers. The list was a who's-who of losers, punks, dopeheads, sleazebags, and skanks—and it was long.

Making mortal enemies is an occupational hazard in the heroin trade.

While we were running through that rogues' gallery, Luther went to another party in Kansas. He met an off-duty prostitute and to impress her, Luther displayed a four-carat diamond ring on his right hand.

"See this ring?" he said. "This is Frankie's eye."

The prostitute, who was no stranger to the heroin market in Colorado Springs, understood that to mean Luther ordered Frankie's assassination and had profited handsomely from the reduction in competition.

Unfortunately, for Luther, the same prostitute was arrested a few days later. She had a record of past offenses and a drug habit. She was only facing a misdemeanor rap, but she preferred her freedom. So she offered her local police department a trade.

She told them about Luther, his ring, and his revenge-killing boast. They called us as a professional courtesy. We jumped on it and soon found others who supported her story.

We obtained a warrant and arrested Luther. In the trunk of his car, we found a paper grocery sack with $260,000 in cash. When I asked Luther about this stash, he said, "Oh, I forgot where I put that!"

I believed Luther on this point. For him, stashing a sack with a small fortune in the trunk was like me leaving loose change in the ashtray. I thanked him for the generous contribution to our police department's seized-assets fund and charged him with murder. Luther is now in prison, where I'm sure business is good, if not quite as good as on the street.

During our investigation, we learned that Luther had paid the two Kansans $250 each, plus gas money, to come to our city and exact revenge on Frankie. Life is cheap in that world.

In fact, I had another revenge motive case in which a local pimp paid two mopes just a hundred dollars to kill a prostitute because she'd been keeping too much of her earnings from him. In this case, gas money was not included, which turned out to work in our favor.

After beating her to death, the two killers put the prostitute's body in the trunk of their car. They were on their way to dump her in the mountains when they stopped for gas. The two mopes argued over who should pay for the fuel. Fists flew.

The gas station owner called the cops. An astute patrol officer spotted blood smeared on the trunk of the car and decided something was amiss. A search revealed the prostitute's body. I had the honor of interrogating Frick and Frack. They weren't shy in offering up the pimp who'd hired them to kill the prostitute out of revenge.

Hiring killers is the same as murder. The pimp went down. He should have thrown in gas money. He paid for it in the end.

Drug-related murders deserve their own category. Sixty-five percent of all homicides involve narcotics in some way, shape, or form. They are a big part of the revenge motive pool because failure to pay and failure to deliver and swiping another guy's stash are all daily events in that low-lying and putrid swamp.

STEWING, FESTERING, AND ERUPTING

Revenge killings, by their nature, are almost always premeditated murders brought about by someone who stewed and plotted for a long time before killing. *You did something bad to me and now I'm going to do something really bad to you. I've thought about this a long time and I'm really going to enjoy killing you because you did me wrong.*

This can go on for years and years. Revenge motive killings often are deeply personal. Many times, the killer and victim were once close friends, or lovers. Family members, too. These are murders cooked on low heat, sometimes over decades.

A guy bought his first car in high school at the age of sixteen. He had planned to drive it to his first prom, but he messed up and his parents grounded him. His best buddy asked if he could borrow the car for that big night, and he agreed.

Then the buddy messed up. He wrecked the car. He apologized many times and paid whatever he could, but forgiveness was not granted. Their friendship disintegrated and rotted into hatred that only grew over the years. Whenever he and his former friend ran into each other, they either argued or fought or both. They became archenemies.

Seven years passed with this gnawing hatred always there. Finally, the owner of the wrecked car could no longer contain his outrage. He shot his former friend in front of an eyewitness, a neighbor. He made no effort to hide it. He couldn't get beyond the pain and suffering his former friend had caused him by wrecking his first car, so he took his life.

All too often, this is what happens in revenge cases. A punch to the face is not enough. The killer feels so betrayed and angry, it is necessary to punish the victim beyond mere eye-for-an-eye retribution. They shoot or stab them multiple times. They beat them to death. Rage erupts. Kill escalates to overkill.

Another pair of high school buddies—you might want to check in with yours just to make sure some old sore point hasn't festered—were about as tight as it gets. Rick and Dave (not their real names) grew up together, went to school together, and even ended up working in the same place.

They double-dated, too. Then Rick found the woman of his dreams and married her. Dave was his best man, naturally. Rick and his bride, Cheryl (also a pseudonym), still saw Dave socially. They even went out with him and one of his girlfriends from time to time. The two guys still worked together, so they saw each other every day.

Everything seemed fine, until Rick came home one day and found a "Dear John" letter from Cheryl. She was divorcing him because she was in love with his best friend and coworker, Dave. Cheryl said she was sorry, but Dave was a better lover, a better guy, a better everything.

Rick was devastated. Cheryl was the love of his life. Things became more than a little awkward at work. Rick and Dave no longer spoke to each other. Cheryl and Dave got married. They still went to the same hangouts where Rick and Cheryl went for years. One night, Cheryl and Dave were at a table in a bar and they saw Rick sitting at the bar by himself. They decided to stay. They drank and they danced. They got a little tipsy. While Dave and Cheryl were dancing, Rick looked their way and, for whatever reason, Cheryl waved at him. Some might have interpreted this as flirting. Others as taunting. Or, to be more generous, maybe Cheryl was simply being kind and friendly to her ex-husband.

Rick seemed to become upset at this. He promptly stood up and left the bar. Then he came back, but now he was wearing a bulky coat. He sat back down at the bar with the coat on and had more drinks.

Dave and Cheryl finally decided to call it a night. They left the bar without saying a word to Rick. He ignored them, or seemed to at first. As soon as they went out the door, he followed them.

He walked up behind them in the parking lot, drew a .357 Magnum from the coat, and shot his former best friend and coworker Dave in the head, killing him.

Then Rick turned to his ex-wife Cheryl and said: "What do you think of that?"

I am not sure what Cheryl thought, though I'm sure she was horrified in that moment and afraid for her own life, too. I thought it was first-degree murder because Rick had obviously planned this out. He'd gone to his vehicle, retrieved the weapon, and concealed it in his coat for a lengthy period of time before following the couple outside and shooting Dave in the head.

His slow-cook revenge had simmered and reached the boiling point when Cheryl smiled and waved at him, for whatever reason. Then Dave died, horribly, in the parking lot and all three lives were destroyed.

Divorce provides fertile ground for revenge. It whips up emotions. The saying is that "revenge is sweet," but it's not sweet. It is hateful, white hot, and explosive. My wife likes this next case, for reasons I will explain later. It involves another divorce that didn't seem particularly heated at first, but then lawyers and judges got involved.

The husband was in the military and based in Colorado Springs. He was what they call "a mustang," which in military parlance means a soldier who started as a low-ranking enlisted man and worked his way up to become a commissioned officer. The term comes from the fact that these are guys who weren't "Thoroughbreds" who graduated from officer's schools or places like West Point. Instead, they were like wild mustangs, who fought and scraped and earned their rank the hard way because they were tough and street smart.

Some mustangs have reached the rank of general over the years, which is quite an accomplishment. One of the most noted mustangs was John William Vessey Jr., a Minnesota guy who enlisted at the age of sixteen in the National Guard and rose to the rank of four-star general and chairman of the Joint Chiefs of Staff. Very impressive!

The Colorado Springs soldier in my investigation reached the rank of army major, which is a very respectable achievement. Just before the major retired, he filed for divorce from his wife of many years. This was in the late 1970s, early 1980s. The law at the time said that women who were divorced from U.S. soldiers did not have any claim on the soldier's retirement benefits. The argument was that the wife hadn't served, so his retirement fund was not part of joint property.

The law is a living, breathing thing that changes. The ex-wife's lawyer fought to get her half of the major's military pension, saying that she was entitled because she'd been married to him his entire military career. A judge in Denver ruled in favor of the major, saying the wife had no claim. The lawyer did what lawyers do. He appealed to a higher court, the Colorado Court of Appeals.

The major thought he was home free, but the appellate court agreed to hear the case, which surprised all parties. They all showed up on the day of the hearing at the federal courthouse in Denver. The ex-wife and her attorney sat up front. The major sat in the back. His attorney called in sick, which pissed him off, apparently.

The appellate court judges, in an unprecedented decision, overturned the existing law and said that the wife was entitled to half the major's pension. This blew out all existing laws pertaining to the protection of the pensions of government employees who divorce.

The major's ex-wife was ecstatic. She hugged her lawyer in the courtroom.

The major was furious. He stormed out.

As the ex and her lawyer walked out of the federal courthouse and started down the steps, the major suddenly appeared and came at them with a drawn .45 automatic. He shot and killed the wife first. Her lawyer went down next.

Then the major hauled ass out of there before anyone could grab him.

We got a call from the Denver Police Department that the major might be headed back our way. Our first thought was that he might be gunning for his own lawyer, who had been sick and not in court that day in Denver.

We warned the lawyer, who lived in our jurisdiction, telling him to stay home. We sent officers to guard him, and we staked out the neighborhood. Sure enough, our guys caught the major just two blocks away. He had his .45 in the car, but he surrendered. He didn't get to enjoy his pension while he served his life sentence.

His wife didn't get the money, either, of course, but her successful appeal was upheld by the U.S. Supreme Court, and as a result, military wives and the wives of all government employees—including Mrs. Kenda—were thereafter entitled to half of the pensions of their husbands if they divorce.

There is a saying that when you seek revenge, you should dig two graves, one for your target and the other for yourself, because the bitterness lives on and destroys you. That was certainly the case for the major and for many others who kill for that motive. In the end, no one wins.

We had a case with an unlikely victim, a middle-class guy with no criminal record or suspicious connections that we could find. He was found shot many times in his own living room. Someone emptied a gun in him, which indicates a crime of passion. The killer likely knew his victim and vice versa.

We brought in friends and family of the victim to see if anything was missing from the house. One of them noticed that a prized autographed baseball was missing from the mantel. We asked around and learned that the victim knew another collector who had sold him the autographed ball and wanted it back for some reason. They had a running feud over it.

I went to the other guy and he confessed right away. In fact, he felt it was justified and didn't see why we were bothering him. He didn't expect to get arrested for killing the guy. He felt justified. He pleaded guilty.

People who kill for revenge expect forgiveness because they think they had a perfectly good reason to take the life they took. They are often quite happy to confess. I've had them say, "What else could I do? He asked for it."

Some revenge killers express pride. I've had a few who didn't mind going to prison. They felt it was worth it. Others probably had their regrets, though I could care less once they are locked up. In this case, we discovered that the autograph on the ball was a fake, so the entire situation was a fiasco. Too bad for both of them. One was dead and the other got life in prison for first-degree murder.

A WOMAN SCORNED

Revenge comes in many forms. Murder isn't always the end result. Sometimes the payback is long-term, and costly. I almost felt sorry for the guy in this case, *almost* being the operative term. He pulled off a pretty spectacular bank robbery in Colorado Springs. Or at least he thought he did. Heck, for a long time *I* thought he'd pulled it off, too.

He showed up at the front door of a downtown bank just before it opened at 9 a.m. He was wearing a business suit and carrying a briefcase. The doors were still locked, but the receptionist saw him standing outside. He was holding up a business card for one of the loan officers.

The receptionist let him in and told him the loan officer would be there in just a few minutes. The guy went to a counter, opened his briefcase, and pulled out a 9mm machine gun. He next pulled out a 36-round clip and inserted it in the machine gun. Then he aimed the submachine gun at the ceiling and emptied the entire clip, shredding the ceiling and light fixtures while scaring the beje-sus out of the bank employees.

He then inserted a fresh 36-round clip in the submachine gun and surveyed the cowering bank staff.

"Now that I have your attention, I want all the money in the bank, or everybody here will die," he said.

They took him seriously.

He walked out with more than $600,000 in cash.

Since the bank wasn't officially open at the time of the robbery, the security cameras had not been turned on. The bank employees had been so frightened they couldn't remember even the color of the robber's hair.

The only evidence we had was the expended bullet casings. You have to jump through a lot of hoops to legally buy a submachine gun in this country. You can do it, but it's a long, drawn-out process and requires a federal tax stamp, so it is all documented. We searched all records for legal sales in the state and then around the country, to no avail. He'd probably bought it on the black market somewhere, or stole it.

We could find no trace of him. We worked the case for two years with no luck.

Then one day, a woman walked into our office.

"Let me tell you about my husband," she said.

You never know where a story might go in these situations, so we listened.

At first, it didn't seem all that interesting: "He has a girlfriend, that fucking bitch . . ."

Then, it did: "He has more than $600,000 cash hidden in the basement because he robbed a bank . . ."

Up to that point, we had nothing on this case. We had no physical description to speak of. No surveillance photos or video. This guy had never had a parking ticket. No criminal record. He was a working-class guy who came up with a plan and pulled off a major bank robbery. He evaded local, state, and federal law enforcement for two years.

I'm sure he'd thought he was home free and financially secure for the rest of his life. But then he went and pissed off his wife by screwing around on her—and she unleashed all her fury, turning the rest of his life to hell.

SEVEN

DRUGS AND DEPRAVITY

You might be tempted to think that killing someone over a baseball or a wrecked car is crazy, but I've seen true depravity, and as a motive for murder, it is in a league of its own. Sometime depravity is triggered by drug or alcohol abuse.

In rare but often high-profile cases, the killer is certifiably insane and driven by demons, whether real or imagined. These are your sociopathic killers, often labeled serial killers. They are headline grabbers featured in magazine articles, books, and scary movies, because they are exceptionally evil.

Gilbert Eugenio Archibeque, twenty-nine, was not a serial killer. He was a "spree killer," according to the website Murderpedia.org. I guess that works, although "spree" makes it sound like killing people was his version of a vacation on the French Riviera.

Gilbert was a once normal and fairly successful guy whose life went down the tubes because cocaine went up his nose. He'd been an Eagle Scout as a kid. He grew up and became a good plumber with a lovely girlfriend. Unfortunately, in the mid-1980s, Gilbert began jamming his own pipes with cocaine. This required him to work extra hours to support his drug habit. Exhaustion set in, and so did paranoia and rage, which are common side effects of cocaine.

As his coke habit grew, Gilbert couldn't fix enough leaky faucets and toilets to pay his dealer. He took a side job as a thief. For his first caper, he put on a mask, grabbed a gun, and robbed the Grand View Lounge, which wasn't far from his apartment.

There was no resistance, and he took home $1,500. Since Gilbert didn't get caught, he thought he'd try it again. He waited about a year before returning.

The owner of the joint, Sonya, had decided in the meantime that keeping so much cash around was a bad idea. She had been making nightly bank deposits instead, cleaning out the cash drawer a few hours before closing, and leaving only a small amount for making change.

Gilbert returned after a Friday night had turned to the first hours of Saturday morning. He expected another good haul, but because Sonya had already been to the bank, the cash drawer contained less than $100.

The lack of more cash may have set off Gilbert's rage. Whatever it was, he shot up the place, killing the bartender and two customers. He clubbed a third customer over the head before shooting him as he crawled under a pool table. The bullet entered and exited the back of that lucky guy's head without causing major damage. He managed to run out the front door and call police.

Gilbert didn't see the survivor. He was too busy setting the tavern on fire. He apparently thought the fire damage might cover up the robbery and murders. Instead of calling it a night, the drug-depraved plumber then went to a nearby convenience store in search of more loot. The clerk there had asked a sister to stay with her because the neighborhood made her nervous. The two of them had heard reports of gunfire coming from the Grand View Lounge and they'd hidden, but Gilbert found them and killed them, too.

When we investigated the murder scene at the convenience store, we found video of Gilbert on a newly installed security camera. He was well known in the area from living and working there. A neighbor recognized him. We had a tactical unit surround his apartment.

Another detective called him on his home phone, told him he was a suspect in several murders, and ordered him to surrender to the officers outside.

He said, "Okay."

Then he turned to his girlfriend, said, "I love you," and shot himself in the head with his .357 automatic handgun. The girlfriend had actually left him because of his cocaine abuse, but she was back in town to visit her mother and had stopped by his apartment. She saw Gilbert kill himself.

I wasn't sad to see him go. In taking his own life, he saved taxpayers a lot of money. We didn't have to pay for his trial and we didn't have to pay to execute him or to keep him locked up for the rest of his life. He also saved a lot of grieving family members an extended period of waiting for their revenge. I hope it helped ease their pain, but it probably did not help much.

COCAINE-FUELED KILLING SPREE

Drugs drove Gilbert Archibeque into depravity. He left five people dead in one night. The prolonged use of cocaine, meth, PCP, heroin, and other addictive stimulant drugs will produce paranoia and fits of rage. Abusing drugs changes your personality. Procuring drugs and using drugs becomes the overpowering purpose in life. Anyone who stands between the user and the drugs is in danger. Psychotic rage builds over time.

I never liked dopers, because they are so dangerously unpredictable. There is no telling what they will do if they can't get the drugs that drive their addictions. Their behavior changes so rapidly that you can get in a real jam with them. For most of their lives, they might have been trustworthy and loving people, like Gilbert the plumber was, but drug use alters their brain chemistry and they become entirely different people. Dangerous people.

Some drugs work faster than other. I've read that 90 percent of people who try meth become addicted after the first use. Breaking any addiction is very, very difficult. Your local librarian who took pain pills because of a bad back can turn into a manipulative and dangerous person once the addiction takes hold.

Some of these drugs, most notably the animal tranquilizer PCP ("angel dust"), and, in more recent years, flakka (made from the stimulant cathinone, found in cheap bath salts), can give their users almost a superhuman strength, which is never a good thing in a raging, drug-seeking maniac.

We were in an emergency room one night with a guy on angel dust, trying to help the medical team subdue him. There were five of us and we couldn't hold down the little guy, who only weighed about 150 pounds. He was throwing us around the room like he was King Kong and we were twigs and branches.

He beat the hell out of us. There was blood everywhere. The PCP freak seemed to get stronger by the minute. We finally pinned him to a gurney and locked restraints on his arms. Then he fought so hard to break free that he broke both his arms.

Drugs turn normal people into zombies. Another time we were in the hospital interviewing someone when a nurse came blasting through the door and said, "There is a guy standing on the trunk of your police car kicking in the back window!"

We ran out and found a guy wearing a hospital gown with his ass hanging out, trying like hell to kick out our squad's rear window. Another druggie. We dragged him off our car and back into the ER. The problem has escalated because so many parents put their kids on Valium or Ritalin and those are gateway drugs. The kids want to try something better that brings them up or down from wherever they are. They move on to painkillers and then cocaine and heroin.

Crack-house raids almost always turned up a couple of suburban kids who'd followed that path, high school and college girls trading sex for drugs, young guys who stole their parents' jewelry to get crack. The drugs take hold of them and become the only thing that matters. If they are awake, they are seeking more. If you get in the way, you could end up dead.

They are crazed by the drugs and they are dangerous, to be sure. Avoid them at all costs. Drugs take a heavy toll mentally and physically. Most are easy enough to recognize, but not always. If you find your neighbor going through your bathroom cabinets, be wary.

THE KILLING KIND

There is another breed of killer apart from all others. You won't spot them easily. They are rare snakes and skilled at camouflage, which makes them all the more dangerous. True psychopathic serial killers can be quite charming, the life of the party, and the death of you.

Only one of them crawled into my career as a homicide detective. His name was Ronald Lee White. He was a drug user, but he murdered because he liked to. He had no qualms about killing on a whim, with guns, knives, and fire. He was an equal opportunity homicidal maniac.

White entered my case files in early 1988, but it took a while to put a name on him. We were called to an apartment complex where a fire had occurred. A seventeen-year-old girl, a martial arts athlete in training for the Olympics, discovered the early morning fire when she'd gone to get a soda from a machine in the complex. She saw smoke coming from under the door of an apartment. She pulled a fire alarm and called 911, saving many lives in the process.

The fire chief said the place was a tinder box and they were lucky to get to the fire before it spread. One resident wasn't so lucky. When firefighters entered the apartment where the fire originated, they found a body. They called us. We determined that the fire had been set to conceal a murder. The nearest smoke alarm had been disabled.

Before the male victim had inhaled any smoke, he'd been butchered with a nine-inch kitchen knife. His perverse killer hadn't stopped there. The victim's intestines had been pulled out of his body and strewn on either side of it, as if for display. Our firefighters were sickened at the sight.

I was taken aback myself. I thought, *Jesus, who are we looking for here, Count Dracula?*

While examining the crime scene, I saw a trail of blood drops on the floor from the body to the kitchen sink. We found a sock in the sink that had been used on a bloody wound, most likely the killer's. I had studied bloodstain pattern analysis and I became known as something of an expert on the topic. Later in my career, I was often called in to consult or testify in court cases about this aspect of crime scene investigation.

This case was before the days of DNA evidence, but it looked like the killer had cut himself while stabbing the victim. The kitchen knife had no hilt like a sword or dagger. It wasn't made for stabbing people, it was made for cutting up steaks. When the killer drove it repeatedly and forcefully into the victim, his hand slipped down to the sharp blade and he cut himself.

We suspected that our killer had a hand wound of some kind. The aspiring Olympian provided us with another clue. She said after pulling the fire alarm, she heard a car in the parking lot start up and leave at a high rate of speed. She only saw it out of the corner of her eye, describing it as a dark-colored sports car with a very loud exhaust sound.

The victim in the apartment was Victor Woods, a bicycle repairman who had been recruited from Ohio to our town by a local bike shop because of his high level of skill. Colorado Springs was a mecca for bicyclists; in fact it's said that you are a true Coloradan if you have a $4,000 mountain bike strapped atop your $800 Subaru.

The question of the day was, Who would so maliciously maim and murder this well-regarded bike repairman? To answer that, we went to work on learning more about him. We found that he was a single guy, and like a lot of single guys, on his paydays he'd go to a local bar, in his case the Yukon Tavern, to drink, play pool, and listen to music.

A woman bartender there told us that on the night of his murder, Woods drank too much and recognized that he shouldn't drive. He asked her for a ride. She offered to call a cab for him, but he said he'd spent all of his money. The bartender was mulling that over when another guy sitting at the bar offered to give Woods a ride home.

The woman bartender remembered the guy, saying he was a good-looking dude, even "movie star handsome." She recalled something else that struck a familiar note with me. She said that a few minutes after the two customers walked out, she heard a car with a very loud rumbling exhaust start up and leave the parking lot of the bar. She did not see the car, but she remembered that it sounded like a hot sports car of some kind.

This matched up with the recollection of the Olympic martial arts athlete who discovered the fire in the victim's apartment. Maybe, just maybe, our killer had a hot rod. It wasn't a great lead, but it was all I had. I told my fellow detectives and officers to make contact with the local sports car clubs, hot rod mechanics, and body shops. We were looking for a handsome guy who drove a hot car with a loud exhaust.

As I said, it wasn't a great lead. Three months passed without a break in the case. One morning, I went into work early, before anyone else, and, following my usual routine, I made coffee and then sat down at my computer to read the daily reports from other police agencies. First, I'd read what had come in on the federal law enforcement wire. These included reports on wanted criminals and their modus operandi, unidentified bodies that had been found, and suspected criminal operations including car theft rings and other scams.

Once I finished the federal report, I looked at the overnight material sent to us by the Rocky Mountain Information Network, made up of law enforcement agencies in our region. I was scrolling through screen after screen until I came upon a report from the Pueblo Police Department. Pueblo is just forty-five miles south of Colorado Springs on Interstate 25, so we often deal with the same criminal element.

Our bad guys headed down there to commit crimes and hightail it back. Their bad guys visited our town to commit crimes and hightail it back. They had to drive through Wigwam, which was halfway between our two cities, but that little bump in the road never seemed to slow them down much.

I was on my second cup of coffee by the time I saw the Pueblo PD report that made my morning. The report said they'd arrested a suspect in a murder and robbery at a Pueblo hotel. He'd shot a hotel clerk in the forehead with a large-caliber handgun, killing him. A security guard showed up and confronted him. The armed robber shot him in the chest, but he survived. The security guard told Pueblo PD that the shooter was a good-looking guy driving a dark blue Chevy Camaro.

Their detectives tracked him down and arrested one Ronald Lee White. The mug shot showed him to be the tall, dark, and handsome sort that a woman bartender might remember. The report said Pueblo PD had impounded the suspect's car. I sent our guys to check it out and to make a sound recording of its engine and exhaust. It was dark blue, in cherry condition, rebuilt with a frame-off restoration and glasspack mufflers loud as shit.

I called Pueblo detectives and inquired about their suspect. They said he was a cold-blooded motherfucker who refused to talk. He was from Indiana originally, but had lived all over the country, a drifter. His last job was selling tanning beds, which were all the rage back then. He'd bought the Camaro just recently and it was his pride and joy.

KILLER ON THE ROAD

Both his parents were dead—of natural causes. I checked. He had a sister back in Indiana who wanted nothing to do with him. She said he didn't care about anyone. Surprisingly, White didn't have a criminal record, other than some juvenile busts for assault and other petty stuff. A lot of people get in trouble when they are kids, so I didn't make much of that.

Things got even more interesting when Pueblo detectives told me that they'd added another murder charge to White's court file. He'd had a roommate who'd shared his apartment for three years. The roommate, Paul Vosika, had disappeared in late August or early September of 1987, according to family members. White initially said Vosika had moved out of town. In May 1988, a portion of Vosika's skull, with the jawbone and teeth intact, was found in Rye Mountain Park, near Pueblo. Searchers found plastic bags nearby that contained a knotted cord, a pair of black leather gloves, and a miter saw. Later, White confessed to the Pueblo PD that he'd killed his roommate, too.

This guy wasn't going anywhere , based on the murder charges, so I asked Pueblo PD to bring him to Colorado Springs for a talk; I had a strategic purpose. It's about an hour drive. I wanted Ronald

Lee White in his handcuffs and orange jumpsuit to wonder during that drive why a detective in Colorado Springs wanted to talk
to him.

If White was guilty of killing the bike mechanic, I wanted him
stewing over it. I wanted the images of his victim, the blood and
carnage, fresh in his mind and haunting him. That ploy might have
worked on 98 percent of the murderers I'd brought in, but Ronald
Lee White was not like any killer I'd ever encountered.

I watched through the two-way mirror as they brought him
into my interview room and he seemed to fill it up. Big hands and
wrists so thick that his handcuffs were on the first click, as wide as
they could go. He was an imposing guy, muscular, with a cold confidence, flashy smile, and eyes that were like staring into a dark pit
with no bottom. There was no shine to them at all. They were dull
and cruel.

I could see him. He could not see me. My first impression was
that my plan to make him anxious on the drive to Colorado Springs
had failed miserably. He seemed bored to death.

I left him alone to simmer in his boredom for a while, hoping
maybe he'd get worried during the wait if I gave him time to fret
over why he'd been hauled into my jurisdiction.

I let him stew for an hour, or at least that was my plan. When I
came back, he was asleep with his head on his forearm on the table,
like a teenager napping during study hall.

Cocaine was supposedly his drug of choice. If I hadn't known
that, I would have suspected Zoloft or Valium. He was facing murder
raps in one town. He was hauled off without explanation to another
jurisdiction. And he's sound asleep in my interrogation room?

This is a cold-blooded reptile, I thought.

He woke up when I walked in and sat down. I asked if he knew
why I'd brought him in from Pueblo.

No.

I explained our investigation into the murder of bike repair-man Victor Woods and the suspicious fire in his apartment complex.

No response. White appeared to wallow in his apathy.

I then told him that in our investigation, we learned that Woods had been drinking at the Yukon Tavern and received a ride home that night from a guy with a hot car like his. Something went wrong after they reached the apartment, I explained, and the guy who gave the bike mechanic a ride home stabbed him and viciously cut him open. On his way out, the killer disabled the fire alarm and set a fire to cover up the murder, I said.

"The killer figured nobody saw him, but he was wrong," I said. "Someone did see him and they saw his slick Camaro, too. They saw him start it up and drive away."

No response. White's level of boredom seemed to have subsided, just slightly. He wasn't sweating it.

This guy has no conscience, no soul, and certainly no heart, I thought.

I saw his eyes take in the "No Smoking" sign in the interrogation room.

"You smoke?" I asked.

"Yeah," he said. "But then there's that sign."

"I kind of run the place," I said. "Let me get you some smokes and an ashtray."

I pushed the pack to him. His hands were cuffed in front of him so he could reach it and open them. He stuck a cigarette in his mouth. I held up a plastic lighter and then tossed it to him.

He caught it with his right hand.

It was a Sherlock moment.

Victor Woods was stabbed by a right-handed killer, according to the coroner's report. Another clue: White had to open his right hand to catch the lighter. When his fingers drew back, I saw a nasty scar in the palm, a linear pink scar that looked only a few months old.

I reached across the table and pointed to the scar.

"You got that when you killed Victor, didn't you?"

"Yeah, and it fucking hurt," he said without emotion.

Game over, and he couldn't have cared less.

Now we were like two guys bullshitting in a bar, and I do mean bullshitting. White would become well known for offering different versions of his murderous tales. Initially, he told me that Victor Woods offered him a beer in exchange for the ride home, and when they were in the apartment, Woods made a sexual advance, according to White.

I called bullshit and White backed away from that claim, saying he decided to kill Woods "because he was an asshole."

He said he grabbed a kitchen knife and stabbed him.

"Why did you cut open his stomach and pull out his guts?" I asked.

"I was just curious. I thought it was cool," he said.

Since Ronnie was on a roll, I asked about his missing roommate.

"I killed that motherfucker, too," he said.

Giving White a cigarette seemed to light his fuse. Eventually he would offer several wildly different accounts of why and how he killed Paul Vosika. He told Pueblo PD and others that they had argued over drugs, or over drug payments and over debts owed.

The version he gave me wasn't about drugs or money. It was about *Star Trek*.

It seemed cocaine wasn't White's only addiction. He was also addicted to the original *Star Trek* television series. He'd found a cable channel that ran the old episodes on Sunday afternoons. He'd sit and drink and watch a marathon featuring Captain Kirk, Mr. Spock, and the crew of the Starship *Enterprise*.

In his statement to me, White claimed that Vosika walked in and changed the channel from *Star Trek* to an NFL game without saying "Mother, may I?"

Pissed, White went to his room, grabbed his gun, and shot his roommate in the back of the head. Some might say this was an over-reaction, but we are talking about a cold-blooded psychopath here. He didn't need a good reason to kill someone, or any reason at all.

After murdering Vosika, White wrapped his body in a shower curtain and hauled it off in his victim's own pickup truck, because, as he told me, he didn't "want to fuck up my Camaro." Again, White has given various accounts of what followed in interviews with others. The version he gave me was that he took the body to a state park outside Pueblo, where he planned to cut it up with a saw and bury it in scattered places. He was just getting started when a couple pulled up in a car next to the truck. They couldn't see the body in the pickup bed.

They were lost and wanted directions out of the park.

White told me that he briefly considered killing them and their child in the backseat. He even had it planned that he would kill the kid in front of them to make the parents suffer before killing them. Apparently, this was just a fleeting thought. That unsuspecting family barely escaped joining White's list of victims.

Deciding that he already had enough on his plate, White gave them directions to the exit, watched them leave, and went to work cutting up the body and dispersing it. As he weaved his tale, there was no emotion in his voice. No light in his eyes. I could feel the rage in him all the same.

White claimed to me and others that he committed at least fifteen murders, maybe as many as twenty-three. I'm sure he would have killed me during our interview if he'd had the chance. Life means nothing to psychotic killers like Ronald Lee White, not even his own.

He was sentenced to death, but that sentence was commuted. White then asked the court to reinstate his death sentence. So far, he remains alive, incarcerated, and probably frustrated that he hasn't pulled off one final killing.

Few killers have left such a lasting impression on me. White is evil incarnate and all the more dangerous because he masked his true nature with considerable charm, much like Ted Bundy, the serial killer and rapist who was executed after confessing to thirty murders.

For a while, White was represented by a public defender who hated me. She thought *I* was evil incarnate because I'd put so many of her clients behind bars. Even though her client was a confessed killer, this attorney gave *me* death looks whenever we crossed paths.

I was always extremely cordial to her, because I knew it pissed her off.

"Your hair looks lovely today," I'd say.

She'd get so pissed at me, her whole body would quiver in anger.

I was visiting the county jail one day when the booking desk officer reported that this public defender was there to talk to her client Ronald Lee White. I tracked her down outside the interview room and offered a warm greeting: "How are you doing?"

Once again: the Death Stare.

I ignored this and offered her a word of warning, just to keep our love alive.

"You can take this advice or leave it, but when they bring White down for your meeting, don't let them leave you alone with him and don't ever get within his reach. He really is Hannibal Lecter."

She gave me the same hateful glare, but I could see a flicker of fear behind her death-ray vision.

She then walked into the interview room alone, despite my thoughtful advice.

Thirty minutes later, I saw her leaving in a mad dash for the front door of the jail. She was ghostly pale, as if she'd had an encounter with Satan himself.

As she blasted out the door, I asked in a concerned tone, "Did you have a bad experience?"

She did not respond, but she later withdrew as White's defense attorney and another public defender took her place on his team.

If the eyes really are the window into the soul, Ronald Lee White's were the exception. His offered only a view of his dark and barren emptiness. Looking into his eyes was like looking through his head into blackness. I've never known anyone like him in that regard. White was wickedness in human form.

PART III

CATCHING KILLERS

EIGHT

I TALK TO DEAD PEOPLE

Murder scenes were always chaotic when I arrived. The bigger the case, the crazier they were. If it was a major headliner, all the big shots showed up to dance in the limelight, city officials, politicians, and police brass among them. Even a run-of-the-mill murder scene would be packed with fire department EMTs, the coroner's team, newspaper and radio reporters, television crews, and crime bloggers. Neighbors, family members, and rubberneckers completed the twelve-ring circus.

Everyone wanted to yap in my ears. I just wanted to catch the bad guy.

TV reporters demanded a comment because they were going live at ten and the earth would stop revolving if I didn't give them a sound bite. If it bleeds, it leads in their world. The ink-stained newspaper wretches pleaded for a few words before the deadline so they'd be spared an ass-chewing from their editors.

This extraneous madness created the Tower of Babel effect. You could not hear yourself think amid the chaos. I needed to think, so I'd keep walking through the roaring scrum, ignoring the press and the onlookers.

In the movies and television shows, this was where I should have locked eyes with the crazed and drooling killer, blood dripping from pant legs as he lingered in the crowd to admire his handiwork.

That never happened to me. It was never that easy.

I'd just keep walking, looking ahead, taking in only what was relevant to the investigation. I took the most direct path to the victim. As I approached the crime scene, I consciously entered into a zone, focusing my mind, tightening down the screws.

My process was always the same. As I stepped under yellow tape, I'd take a deep breath. Then I'd flip the switch on my hearing to shut out the din on the other side of the yellow tape. The yapping, the clicking camera flashes, and the scratching and squawking of emergency radio traffic . . . it all became white noise.

I'd turn off my pager and leave my two-way in the car. *Leave me alone. Let me do my job.*

I'd beat feet to the working side of the yellow police tape as quickly as I could. There I'd find quiet, and at least one dead person, sometimes more. Once I was in the zone, the questions came. *How did the killer get here? Was there forced entry? Did someone let in the killer? Was the door unlocked or locked?*

Many things were possible. If it was forced entry through a door or window, that indicated it might have been a stranger, possibly a burglar who discovered someone was home and killed them.

Absence of forced entry is important. It suggests different scenarios. It implies, not conclusively, that the victim might have known the killer and let them in. The other possibility is that the door wasn't locked and the killer just walked in.

A uniformed cop was usually posted at the entrance. His job was to tell me where the victim was located. *Living room,* he'd say. Or, *Kitchen to the right.* I registered his words while taking in everything I could see. I was looking for anomalies, evidence of things disturbed or missing. Knocked over lamps, drawers pulled out, pillows or magazines or knickknacks scattered on the floor. *What is odd here?*

I'd take into account that maybe messy was normal in this domicile. It could belong to a contender for the world's worst housekeeper. More people live in squalor than you might imagine, and not all of them do so because they are poor, uneducated, or out of their minds on drugs. Rich people can be slobs, too.

Still, clothing scattered everywhere on the floor could be normal, or it might indicate a struggle, or a search. All of this channeled through my mind as I walked to the victim's location. Once I reached the body, gears switched. The person who once existed within the body became the focus of my observations and my questions.

I looked at the dead person and I addressed my questions directly to that victim. *What happened to you? Can you tell me? Maybe you can . . .*

Crime scenes whisper to you, but you have to be smart enough to listen.

If the victim's eyes were open, and sometimes they were, I looked into them and said, "You know you can't see me, but maybe you can hear me. I'm here to find out who did this to you, and I assure you I will. Tell me, if you don't mind, how did you die?"

It can be sobering and bizarre to share space with a corpse that until very recently was somebody's child, spouse, friend, or coworker. I am always reminded that my investigation has meaning for all of the victims and those who loved and cared for them.

Even so, I learned early on to tamp down my emotions and remain calm inside the yellow tape. *What is done is done. We can't undo this. We can't bring this person back to life. It has been taken away forever. What we can do is find who is responsible for the death in our midst. I want to give the killer a face and a name. I want the murderer brought before the bar of justice to answer why this life was taken. I can do that, but not if I hurry too much, overlook evidence, and make hasty assumptions.*

ALONE WITH A CORPSE

I talked to dead people because it helped me enter the proper mental state. I was there for the victims. I wanted to honor their lives by solving their deaths. I asked them what happened. No answers were expected, at least not audibly. They told me a lot by their body positions, the amount of blood lost—where it went and the pattern it made—the state of decomposition, the presence of defensive wounds, the items and clothing on the body or missing from it.

What can I tell from your injuries? Are your wounds on the front of your body, the back, or both? Did you die in a defensive position as if you saw death coming? Or were you relaxed and unaware? Are there defensive wounds on your body that indicate a struggle to the death? Is there bruising or redness around the neck to indicate that hands or a rope or belt were on your throat?

What was the cause of your death? The weapon used?

Identifying the weapon was a priority. The possibilities were endless. Guns, knives, ashtrays, and baseball bats were the most common instruments of death. Soda bottles and pots and pans were not far behind. If it was a stab wound, I looked to determine what kind of blade went through the flesh. If the wound remained open, I pressed it closed with my fingers, wearing gloves, of course.

A standard knife has one sharp edge and narrows to a fine point like a triangle. A knife meant to be a weapon will usually have two sharp sides. You can tell by the wound which sort of knife it was.

The number of wounds is important also because it indicates the emotional state of the killer. One or two wounds indicates that killing the victim was enough. If the victim has been shot six or eight times, or stabbed multiple times, there is rage and hatred in play.

Strangulation is also an indication of great hatred and anger. *I am strangling your ass because I want to watch you die. I want to see the light go out in your eyes.* This is a killer who is very close to the victim. This could be personal, just as a gunshot at close range can indicate that the killer was delivering a message, not just murdering the victim but making a statement.

Choking someone to death is not easy. The muscles of the neck are among the toughest in the body. To overcome them and compress the airway requires great force and it takes two minutes or more of clamping down. You have to maintain that grip while the victim is fighting for his life. This is very personal. *I am not going to let up or stop because you are struggling. I am determined to kill you in one of the worst and most personal ways possible.*

KEYS TO THE CRIME

My job was to answer the *Who, What, Where, When*, and *How* questions at every crime scene. As I noted earlier, the *Why* question, the motive behind the murder, is important only if it leads to the *Who*. Really, once I knew the *Who*, I did not care about the *Why*. That was a question for the jury or the judge to explore.

After I'd badgered the poor victim's body with questions, I would turn the focus of my postmortem inquiries to the only other person who knew what had happened: the suspect. These questions were asked in absentia, of course. If the killer had been standing there, my job would have been a whole lot easier, but so damned boring.

The other cops present often worried that I'd blown out a frontal lobe when I asked questions of the suspect into thin air. *What did you do in here? What did you do? When you decided that this person at my feet had to die. How did you accomplish that? Did you bring a weapon with you? Did you use it and remove it for further use? Or was this a weapon of opportunity? Did you take it from the house, or did you deposit it somewhere nearby?*

Let's consider that maybe when you arrived here, you did not intend to kill this person. Maybe something went wrong. Something triggered your anger. Maybe you grabbed the nearest item you could find and used it to end the life of this person. What was it? Where did it go after the killing was done?

In stabbings, I always looked for a kitchen knife block to see if any part of the set was missing. Then I'd look in the sink and the dishwasher to see if any knives were freshly washed. Trash and garbage cans were always worth a search.

If the killer brought the weapon with him, that is malice aforethought; a plan was in place. But if the murderer came in without a weapon, only to fly into a rage, it opened other possible scenarios.

The questions I asked were based on observation and common sense, which are a detective's best tools. A solid grasp of human nature is also an asset. I don't claim to understand people, but they do interest me. They usually behave in predictable ways. No one likes to think that is true of them, but it is.

Killers like to think they are clever, but most follow basic patterns. Looking at the aftermath of most murders, I could pick out basic patterns and choose between them. Those patterns reveal themselves through observations of the crime scene. Someone came to commit murder, or when they came they were compelled to murder.

Many cases in private homes revolve around proprietary interest. The victim possesses something that the killer wants, or claims ownership of. The visit is made to reclaim that property. The death results when the killer decides murder is the only way to get it back.

This type of scenario is common, which is why it is important to look around each room to see if anything of value appears to be missing. Is there something missing from a spot on the wall? A dust-free empty space on the mantel or bookshelf? We may also ask a friend or family member to check for missing items. That is how we discovered the missing (fake) autographed baseball in the case I mentioned earlier.

TRAINING THE EYE AND THE MIND

Let's go back to the photograph I used in my police academy training classes for young detectives. The female victim had been shot multiple times in the center of her chest. Closer observation revealed that the killer put a pattern of shots in her. He was either a marksman or standing at close range. And he was engaging in overkill.

One bullet to the chest should have sufficed if this was a simple street robbery. Two shots would have definitely done the job. Yet he emptied the gun into her. Continuing to fire every round into a prone and mortally wounded body indicates rage. It would also seem to tell us that there was a connection between the victim and her killer. To hate her that much, he must have known her.

Since she was shot in public on a city street, we might conclude that our killer was acting impulsively, out of emotion, rather than calculation. A more calculated move would have been to kill her in a place with fewer potential witnesses. This is another indicator that the killer knew her.

You can't draw conclusions from all that information, but you can find a direction for your investigation. We don't know why she was killed, but we had some evidence that her killer knew her and was angry enough to kill her.

We have more questions than answers at this point. Who is this victim? Is she married? Divorced? Where does she work? Where does she shop? Who are her best friends? Who are her enemies? What are her habits, hangouts, and hang-ups? Any dark secrets, like alcoholism, an addiction to painkillers, or sexual adventures? Does she owe a bundle of money to someone?

SOMETIMES IT IS WHAT IT SEEMS

I always kept an open mind, but my standard approach was to start with the most likely scenarios, such as a jealous husband or lover, a rival in love or at work, a spurned suitor, a stalker, or a feuding family member. If none of them panned out, then I'd move to the fringes and consider a robbery or rape that escalated into murder, or a spur-of-the-moment act of violence, and go down the list from there.

In this case, the most likely scenario proved to be true. This was a domestic homicide motivated by the husband's jealousy based on unproven suspicions. He believed she was cheating on him, but, by all accounts, she was not.

Paranoia and rage led him to shoot her on a public street. This is rather typical of the abusive male personality. They had long-simmering problems over his unfounded accusations. She could do nothing to convince him otherwise. She died, innocent to the end. He was found guilty and went to prison for life.

That case, as with most, proved to be exactly what it seemed. Still, you can't assume anything going into an investigation. Even the simple ones can throw in unexpected twists and turns, especially when the crime scene becomes contaminated.

I was in charge of the detective division and in my unmarked car when one of my guys called on a scrambled two-way channel that the press can't monitor. He'd gone to check out a suspected suicide, which is part of the job. Something wasn't looking right. He asked me to come take a look.

There was an emergency ambulance parked out front. They were waiting for me to examine the scene before they removed the body. I walked inside. The apartment looked like a monk's place, sparsely furnished, a simple bed with no linens. The body was prone and faceup on a mattress, with a gunshot wound to the mouth. The former contents of his head were blasted on the wall behind him.

Looked like a suicide, but there was one problem.

"I don't see a gun," my detective said.

The lack of a weapon would complicate things. I've yet to meet a gun with legs. They don't walk off on their own. Unlike what you might see on television crime shows, however, it is extremely rare to find the gun still in the hand of a true suicide. As I noted earlier, the muscles in the hand relax upon death and the weapon usually falls somewhere nearby. If it isn't there, someone moved it, or caused it to move.

"Ask the EMTs if anyone knelt on the bed while they were checking his vitals," I said.

I'd seen cases where the EMT kneels on the bed, compresses the mattress, and knocks the gun to the floor, or under the bed, or under the victim himself. They weren't supposed to do that, but in their haste to get to the victim, they sometimes did.

When we searched under this victim's body, we found a 9mm cocked and ready to rock. Not a good thing. He'd fired one shot and then the gun fell from his hand onto the mattress beside him. It had shifted beneath him when the EMTs did their initial check.

So, it was a suicide, easy enough. Still, there was another twist awaiting in this case. When I turned the head of the victim, I got a look at what remained of his face. There was enough left for me to recognize it as familiar. I didn't need much to work with because most of the time when I'd seen this guy he wore a surgical mask anyway.

A FAMILIAR FACE

This was someone who'd had his hands in my mouth. I'd spit in a cup for him. He was my dentist, with the emphasis on the *was*. I was sad to see him go, but not all that torn up that my upcoming appointment would have to be canceled. I hate going to the dentist. Doesn't everyone?

I liked this guy, though. He was personable. Like most dentists, he was a good model for his own work, flashing perfect teeth at his cavity-prone patients. I was not surprised to observe that he'd taken great care of his teeth even as he blew out the back of his head. He'd made sure to bite down on the gun barrel so the bullet did not nick his pearly whites. Impressive, but sad.

His office was on speed dial so I called and asked for his partner.

"He's with another patient," said the receptionist.

"I'm not calling as a patient," I said. "I'm calling as a cop. This is an emergency. Go get him."

He stopped drilling and came on the line. I gave it to him straight up.

"I am at your partner's apartment. He is deceased from single gunshot wound to the mouth."

He dropped the phone and had to retrieve it.

The partner was hyperventilating when he came back on the line. I gave him a minute and then offered free legal advice.

"If you have a survivor clause in your partnership agreement, you need to close your joint accounts. And you need to notify your staff."

While I had him on the phone, I asked if he had any idea why his partner might take his own life. He explained that despite all I'd paid him, my dentist had financial problems. He'd lost nearly $900,000 in a bad investment scheme. His wife had kicked him out.

I'd always found him to be a very upbeat, charming guy. Their office was very busy. He was in his early forties and seemed to have it made, but dentists have the highest rate of suicide of any occupation. You'd think it would be cops or morgue attendants because of all the depressing shit they have to deal with. There must be something depressing about looking into people's mouths every day. Losing nearly a million dollars and your wife might do it, too.

MESSY BUSINESS

Aside from the "missing" weapon and my personal connection to the suicidal dentist, this was a fairly typical crime scene. Meaning it was a mess. First of all, there were just too damned many people allowed within the yellow tape. Years ago, fire departments realized that there were fewer fires due to safer buildings and fire alarms and fewer people smoking cigarettes in bed. So, to justify their numbers and the insurance rates, fire departments turned most of their people into emergency medical technicians, or, as I call them, "almost doctors."

Our crime scenes became even more congested after that. All the emergency personnel tended to fuck up the investigation by tromping all over the place, spewing gauze, bandage wrappers, IV lines, and their fingerprints on top of the perpetrator's. When this problem first arose, I made a point to go around to fire stations and ambulance companies, asking them to be aware of the importance of preserving evidence and the scene of the crime.

They didn't pay much attention. So, when I found bloody footprints from their boots and shoes all over my crime scenes, I'd have the crime scene techs take photos of the souls of all their shoes so we could use the photos to eliminate footprints from our investigation.

The EMTs and firefighters did get better at not messing up after years of hearing me complain. Now they are trained more thoroughly to be unobtrusive, but another problem came up when hospitals developed emergency medical protocols that basically said that they had to bring in the victim from the scene, even if there were no vital signs, so that resuscitation could be attempted. The only exceptions were if the body had been decapitated, severely dismembered, or so decomposed there was no chance for survival.

This was understandable. They were trying to err on the side of caution. I've seen victims whose breathing was so shallow you couldn't detect it easily. It's also true that medical training and technology has come a long way and they can "bring back" patients who never would have made it back in the old days.

The body was almost always headed to the morgue by the time I arrived at the crime scene later in my career. That made it tougher to do a thorough investigation. Your favorite cop shows and movies always have a body at the scene, but it's increasingly rare in real life.

Most of what you see in shows like *CSI: Dubuque* or wherever is pure fantasy. Just a few months ago, a friend of mine who is a homicide detective called me with a funny story about the gap between television crime scene investigators and the real thing. His detectives had a protracted murder case involving gang members. Charges were filed and the case went to the jury. The jurors spent a couple of days sifting through all of the evidence before they sent a note to the judge. They had a question, which is not unusual in a complicated case.

They asked to see the murder weapon, a gun, again, and they asked the court reporter to read back to them a statement made during the trial. All normal stuff. But then the foreman of the jury sent the judge a note asking why a certain test hadn't been done on the murder weapon.

The judge said it hadn't been done because there was no such test. It didn't exist.

The jury foreman replied, "Well, they have it on *CSI*."

CSI ON TV IS BS

Sorry to report also that real-life female cops, crime scene investigators, and technicians don't show up with five-hundred-dollar hairdos, four-inch heels, and button-busting tight blouses. They do not look like they've just come from competing in beauty pageants or a Victoria's Secret catwalk. They are professionals and they dress the part. If they showed up looking like glamour queens, they'd get sent home or laughed out of the room by their coworkers. It's not glamorous work. It's bloody, smelly, and gritty business.

Oh, another thing you won't find at real crime scenes: chalk outlines of the body's location. I think that was last done in the 1930s. And while crime scene investigation has come a long way thanks to modern science, real CSI team members don't carry badges or guns and they don't chase down suspects like they are Dirty Harry.

That's the job of the homicide detectives and their fellow officers. CSI people are mostly science nerds. Not bloodhounds. More like lab rats. Their supervisors have doctorates. They have government-issued microscopes, not Glocks, and they don't interrogate suspects.

My interaction with crime scene techs was usually limited to "Make sure you get that print and pick up that brain matter on the wall." I'd hunt. They'd gather. Most of them smelled like your first chemistry set.

The few *CSI* television shows I've seen have crime labs that look like something you could fly to Mars and back in a couple of hours. Real crime labs aren't that high-tech because they are funded by local, state, and federal governments. The average police department can't afford a crime lab so they send anything found at the crime scene to places like the FBI lab in Quantico, Virginia.

Most city detectives can only pray that they get test results back before they die of old age. If you are a sheriff in rural Wyoming with six deputies and responsible for an area the size of Rhode Island, and nothing much happens except cattle rustling and snake bites, you don't have your own forensics lab. If you find a young woman raped, murdered, branded, and displayed for all to see in a cow pasture, you've got public outcry and a big case on your hands.

That sheriff may decide to get the best forensic help possible, so he collects blood, semen, and all the other evidence he can gather and calls the only public crime lab available to him, the FBI lab in

Quantico. He explains to the FBI employee who answers the phone the heinous murder and the importance of his case.

And this is the response he gets: "How many victims were there?"

"Just one."

"I'm sorry, we only accept cases with multiple victims."

Click.

Quantico doesn't have time for the small stuff. They are buried in multiple homicide cases. Another thing about CSI as portrayed on television that is so insane: the technology they carry around, all those magical tools that no real cops have ever seen or imagined. The TV guys always seem to get fingerprint and DNA results within a few seconds, if not after the next commercial for male impotency. These days in Colorado, if you put a rush on a DNA sample, you'll be lucky to get it back in nine months.

FINGERPRINTS SMUDGED

Yes, the federal government has AFIS, the Automated Fingerprint Identification System, which is contained in a $640 million super-computer in Clarksburg, West Virginia. As with all computer-based systems, AFIS is only as good as the information entered into its data banks. Fingerprints gathered by law enforcement agencies nationwide are entered as time and budgets allow, but they don't have every print left by every criminal ever hauled in for questioning or an arrest.

On television, they submit a fingerprint and within seconds their super-duper computers cough up the suspect's photo, current location, blood type, hat and ring size, and stomach contents. I may be exaggerating, but you have to admit, it's ridiculous, and totally fiction.

In the real world, you submit a set of prints and within a couple of weeks or months AFIS sends you back fifteen possible suspects. Fingerprints don't tell you who the suspect is so much as they tell you who it isn't. Without much effort, most decent defense attorneys can chew up and spit out fingerprint evidence as worthless.

Fingerprint evidence was championed by longtime FBI chief J. Edgar Hoover, who was the consummate bureaucrat. Before fingerprints, they were relying on knee prints, elbow prints, ear prints, claiming that all were unique to each of us and that the minute differences permitted identification of suspects.

Common sense dictated that fingerprints became the key because criminals had to use their hands and fingers in most crimes. The standard for identification was finding twelve points on the suspect's finger that were identical to the latent print. That number was picked at random. In Europe, they need eighteen points to establish identity.

The problem is that fingerprint examinations are based more on opinion than science. There have been many cases that proved this, but one of the most powerful examples was the subject of a very good investigative piece by the PBS program *Frontline*. I'd heard about the case before *Frontline* did the story, as had most people in law enforcement.

The story sprang from the terrorist attack in Madrid, Spain, in March 2004. Attackers bombed a passenger train and killed 191 people. The Spanish national police found eight latent prints at the bomb site. Through Interpol, they sent digital images of them to the FBI's AFIS for identification, which at the time had some 48 million prints on file. AFIS spit out the names of more than a dozen individuals as possible matches.

FBI examiners claimed that a print on a plastic bag containing bomb detonators found at the scene had fifteen points of similarity with those of a U.S. lawyer, Brandon Mayfield, thirty-seven, of Portland, Oregon. This implied that Mayfield was at the scene of the bombing and involved in it. Suspicions were elevated because the lawyer was a former U.S. Army lieutenant, who had married an Egyptian, converted to Islam, and was handling a child custody case for one of the Portland Seven, a group convicted of trying to travel to Afghanistan to help the Taliban.

Mayfield maintained his innocence, noting that he didn't even have a passport and hadn't been overseas in more than ten years, but things weren't looking good for him. If convicted, he could have faced the death penalty.

His hide was saved because Spanish investigators disagreed with the FBI's claim that his prints were a 100 percent match. They'd found eight points of similarity, but several dissimilarities as well. The Spaniards refused to charge Mayfield. Instead, they kept looking at other suspects.

The FBI then had a fourth examiner take a look and he ruled that there was a Mayfield match. Agents took Mayfield into custody under the Patriot Act as a "material witness," without charging him. They initially would not allow him to see his family yet refused to say why he was being detained. He hired a team of lawyers, who in turn hired a forty-year FBI veteran who served as head of their fingerprint division. They asked him to examine and compare the prints. He said they belonged to Mayfield, too, much to the consternation of the suspect and his legal team.

Their worries ended, however, when a short time later the Spanish version of the FBI identified the fingerprints found on the bag of detonators as belonging to one Ouhane Daoud, an Algerian, who had similar detonators in his possession when they nabbed him. The Spaniards said Daoud, not Mayfield, was the terrorist whose prints were on the bag found at the scene.

The FBI sent its fingerprint experts to Madrid so they could get a firsthand look at the original print. Close, but no cigar, they said. The two men had very similar fingerprints, but the FBI admitted that they'd been wrong. They blamed their mistake on the low-resolution digital print they'd been working with back home.

Brandon Mayfield was handed a get-out-of-jail card and went home with an apology from the FBI. Bad stuff hit the fan when a panel of fingerprint experts ruled that the FBI's bad matchmaking had nothing to do with the quality of the fingerprint photo they'd worked with. Instead, the panel found that the four FBI examiners had ignored dissimilarities between the two prints because of their eagerness to nail a suspected terrorist.

As you might have predicted, Attorney Mayfield filed a lawsuit and won $2 million in damages from U.S. taxpayers. His case also cast substantial doubt on the FBI and its fingerprint analysis expertise. Defense lawyers were ecstatic because for years FBI experts had testified that they had never misidentified a fingerprint match. They weren't telling the truth, and with the Mayfield case, fingerprint evidence would never be so widely trusted.

Before this infamous foulup, an FBI fingerprint examiner would take the stand and say the print submitted as evidence was a match with that of the accused. The jury usually thought since it was the FBI, their testimony had to be correct. That changed, and fingerprint testimony was considered "opinion," not science.

Another problem with fingerprint evidence is that prints look the same whether they are a hundred years old or an hour old. There is no way to determine their age. If you found fingerprints on a letter from Napoleon to Josephine, the experts would have no idea when the print was made. The same can happen in court. A suspect's prints may match those found on a coffee table at the crime scene, but if the suspect had ever been in the house, there is no way to prove when the print on the coffee table was made.

FORSAKEN FORENSICS

Most forensic evidence faces similar problems, whether it is ballistics reports, tire tracks, shoe prints, hair and bite mark comparisons, or findings in an arson case. It's not science so much as opinion, and, as a result, it is often effectively challenged by competent defense attorneys.

I do have faith in the opinions of medical examiners who are doctors and can back up their reports with physical evidence. Most other forensic science leaves me cold. It can be helpful, yes, but you can't build a case on it.

I have found ballistics evidence useful if the gun barrel involved leaves distinctive marks on the bullets recovered at a crime scene. A unique shoe print can also be useful, but knowing that the killer wore size 10-D Nikes is not enough to make my heart go pitty-pat. If you hauled in everyone who wore that size, you'd have a lineup that circled the planet.

Even if the forensics guys can tell me that the Nike-wearing killer knelt down in the victim's blood and left a knee imprint from a pair of Levi 501 jeans, I'm still not getting buzzed. To prove a case, I needed evidence specific to our suspect. Otherwise his defense attorney would saddle me up and ride merrily into the sunset.

Here's an example of a good specific bit of crime scene evidence: A woman was shot. A slug was recovered from her body during the autopsy. The bullet was relatively intact because it didn't hit bone. Our police department's own ballistics expert was well respected in his field. He took a look at it and called me.

"You're a lucky SOB, Kenda," he said.

"Why's that?"

"I will stake my reputation that this bullet was fired from a mint-condition Single Action Army, SAA, Model P, Peacemaker M1873," he said, reveling in his expert glory.

He was talking about the legendary "gun that won the West," a Colt .45, and likely this was a valuable collector's model, worth maybe $12,000.

So, not your typical Saturday night special! This bit of very specific evidence gave me something to chew on. Within a short time,

I found myself talking to an associate of a suspect in the case. He happened to mention that his friend, my suspect, was an antique gun collector.

Excuse me, what did you say? Would you be offended if I kissed you on the mouth?

The rest of the case fell into place, not immediately, but with only a few twists and turns. The owner of the Colt .45 wasn't the killer, but the killer had "borrowed" his prized Peacemaker to disturb the peace and take the life of her handsome lover's poor wife.

I was sad for the victim and her loved ones, but happy that her killer chose such a distinctive weapon, because it helped send the murderous lovers to the hellhole they deserved.

TIGHT GENES ARE THE BEST

The only forensic science that I truly love is that involving DNA evidence, which has been a remarkable boon to law enforcement. DNA testing wasn't developed for detectives. It was created by medical science. We tapped into it after a pioneer geneticist suggested that what worked for him might work for us.

The first cops to use DNA evidence were British detectives in a rural area of England in 1986. They were trying to catch a serial rapist and killer. They had heard of the work done by Alec Jeffreys, an Oxford-trained geneticist at the University of Leicester and a pioneer in the use of DNA to identify kinship in humans.

Jeffreys had given a speech about DNA in which he suggested it could be used in police work to identify suspects. Some in attendance had laughed at him, but the rural police department asked for his help.

They'd investigated two rape-murder cases involving teenage girls that seemed very similar, along with a series of sexual assaults and indecent-exposure incidents in the area. They weren't sure, but they thought one violent sexual deviant might be responsible for most if not all of them.

Local police had identified and questioned a learning-disabled male teen who knew the most recent victim. He'd admitted to the crime a couple of times, but retracted it each time.

Frustrated, they charged him and locked him up to await trial. He maintained his innocence. Police thought he was lying. They were hoping Jeffreys could test semen samples taken from the two victims and identify their suspect as the rapist-killer of both.

The geneticist tested the samples taken from the victims. He immediately realized that both women were raped by the same man, but there was one problem. That man's DNA did not match the learning-disabled suspect in custody.

Jeffreys told the village police they were on the right track, but they had the wrong guy. The British cops then made a big move. They obtained a queen's warrant that allowed them to test every male in the village. They took more than five thousand blood samples from the locals. None of them matched the rapist-killer's DNA.

Their break in the case came a year after the second victim was found. Through an informant, they discovered that one village resident had asked a friend to pose as him when he gave a blood sample. That same resident who evaded testing had been questioned in the first rape and murder.

His name was Colin Pitchfork, a twenty-seven-year-old father of two. When police brought him in for questioning, Pitchfork confessed to both rape-murders as well as two other sexual assaults. He also claimed that he'd exposed himself to nearly a thousand women over the years. The psychiatric report described him as a psychopath with serious sexual perversions. He was sentenced to life in prison.

A BLOODY BREAK

Over the years that followed, Jeffreys developed techniques for DNA fingerprinting and profiling that were soon being used by police departments around the world. I actually had the first Colorado murder investigation in which DNA played a critical role. The murder victim was stabbed to death in 1991. There was blood everywhere and some of it appeared to be from the killer. We had a suspect, a hardened criminal, but he was lawyered up and wouldn't talk.

We had just attended a seminar on the use of DNA in criminal investigations. It was a very new concept—and expensive. As I recall, there was only one company that did testing in the United States and they charged $2,500 for each test. That was a big hit to our department.

The use of DNA for police work at first seemed like a remarkable, magical thing.

We thought it was like science fiction, but we were desperate to solve this case. We'd had one earlier bad experience in which the lab returned no results, so this was a real roll of the dice. The investigation had gone on for more than six years at that point. I'd run out of bullets. I convinced our chief to spend the two and a half grand so we could finally lay the case to rest.

The DNA test nailed the suspect, who flipped on his accomplice. They both pleaded not guilty, but the jury sent them up the river on a slow boat. My bet paid off. I looked like a genius, though in truth, I was just desperate.

Back then, DNA testing was not as sophisticated as it is now and only served as circumstantial evidence. Now it is more definitive when done correctly. Also, the size of the samples needed for evaluation has grown smaller and smaller over the years.

Defense lawyers hate DNA evidence because it is so difficult to counter. Yet there can be problems even with science-based tools.

Those who evaluate DNA samples are often overworked and under stress, not to mention underpaid, especially if they are on the government payroll. Bad apples in crime labs have been known to lie about their qualifications, mix up samples, misinterpret results, and even purposefully misrepresent and falsify findings.

The city of Houston's police department crime lab struggled for years with these problems. Several investigations have uncovered mistakes, ineptitude, and worse since the late 1990s. There were even accusations that some lab workers were acting as "white-coat vigilantes," who decided certain suspects needed to go to prison so they altered DNA results to convict them. Hundreds of "solved" cases have been called into question as a result.

Still, when DNA testing is done properly, it is hard to shake and is the best tool that the science of forensics has to offer. The rest of it can be helpful, but rarely can you build a case around it. If I was still on the job, believe me, I'd still be talking to dead people.

NINE

GUN PLAY

As a rookie patrol officer, I was issued a Smith & Wesson model 19, which is a revolver that holds six rounds, .357 Magnum ammo. Then in the late 1980s the department went to the Smith & Wesson model 5906, which was a 9mm with a 15-round capacity.

These were defensive weapons, for the most part, and the first time someone shot at me on the job, I was definitely on defense. I'd been a cop for six months. I was alone on patrol, and I saw a miscreant yanking the hubcaps off a car and throwing them like he was an Olympic discus wannabe.

My eyes followed the path of flight and I realized he was hurling the hubcaps into the middle of a large crowd in the street outside a notorious joint called the Old Corral.

I had yet to see a law against discus tossing in public, at the public, but that seemed wrong to me.

I jumped out, grabbed the guy, and arrested him before I realized the crowd was actually a huge swarm of fighting drunks. About two hundred enthusiastic and bloody participants had rolled out of the bar while engaged in raging combat.

A riot, in other words.

Like an idiot, I yelled for help. I had no portable radio back then, so I was just yelling in the wind. I'm not sure who I thought would come to help me, the only cop among a scrum of eye-gouging, balls-kicking scumbag gangbangers and cutthroats.

Yep, I was on my own. And yet my mind took me where my body shouldn't go. I waded into the crowd like John Wayne taking on the Comancheros.

The Duke fared much better than I did.

"You are all under arrest," I said.

Exactly no one was impressed, not even when I made it clear that I was a representative of government authority, truth, justice, and the American way.

They were drunk, pissed, and bleeding from their noses. So, they could not have cared less.

There was a scream that rose above the sound of blows and cursing. I turned toward it to behold a guy who had a female in a headlock and a gun pointed at my head.

Finally, someone had noticed me!

"Hey, cop!" he said.

His tone was not welcoming. He was about forty feet from me.

I drew my gun with the rash thought that there was an inch of his forehead clear for a shot. Then I reconsidered; it would be really bad form to shoot the girl instead.

I holstered my weapon. He took careful aim.

I dove down into the street, apparently thinking I could blend in with the pavement like a chameleon.

The muzzle flash was like a bonfire. The gun sounded like a 155mm howitzer artillery piece. It was a .32 automatic, but when someone is shooting at you, it always sounds like the biggest fucking gun in the world.

When I hit the pavement, my head smashed into the street so

hard I blacked out. But as my lights dimmed, I heard sirens in the distance. The cavalry was coming.

A hard poke brought me back. It was a cop with his gun out. He was frantically pushing and probing my uniform: "Joe, where are you hit?"

A motel manager on the midnight shift had looked out the window after giving up on his broken television with rabbit-ear antennae. He'd seen the street fight and then the guy with the gun shooting at me. Being a concerned citizen and otherwise bored, he called it in.

"There's a huge fight in the street here, and a cop just got shot," he'd told our operator.

Nothing orders up a blue-light special more than a report of an officer down. When the first patrolman on the scene asked me where I'd been hit, I told him that I did not know. "The only wet thing I feel is my crotch," I explained. "I don't feel anything else."

We both checked further and found no indications that I'd been aerated.

"You're fine!" he said.

The cleanup lasted until noon. My would-be killer had fled the scene, only to be caught four months down the road. I had reports to write and explaining to do. By the time I headed home I was exhausted and still a little shaky from my near-death experience.

I walked into the house, jittery, ass dragging, and half-asleep.

Out of nowhere came my three-year-old son, Danny, who blasted at me with his toy tommy gun. Battery-operated and loud as hell.

"You're dead, Daddy, I shot you!"

I had the piss scared out of me for the second time in twenty-four hours. My knees went weak. I slid down the wall to the floor and collapsed with my heart doing cartwheels.

"Danny, go to your room," I said feebly. "I've been shot at enough for one day."

UNDER FIRE

There is a never-ending arms race between law enforcement and lawbreakers. Criminals usually had cheap Saturday night specials when I started, but when drugs became prevalent and the major traffickers moved in, they armed their minions with automatic weapons. Once assault rifles started showing up on the street, police departments issued shotguns and semiautomatic rifles to supervisors, and then moved to the M-4, which is a shorter and lighter version of the M-16 assault rifle, so our guys wouldn't be outgunned.

Law enforcement leaders learned their lesson after the 1965 Watts riots, when police officers quickly discovered that the people shooting at them had more firepower. The L.A. cops had to go home and get their hunting rifles and personal weapons to combat what they were up against.

In the late 1960s, police departments built up their armories of weapons and instituted better training in offensive tactics so officers were better equipped and better prepared. Today most patrol cars have a shotgun in a rack next to the driver. Supervisors have racks that carry assault rifles.

All of the weaponry in the world doesn't help if someone catches you by surprise, of course. I once came crashing through the door of a suspect's hiding place, leading my men in the chase. The thug we were pursuing didn't run. He hid behind the door, and as I came through it, he swung at me and hit me in the side.

I smashed him in the face with my gun and turned out his lights. As he went down, I saw he had a small knife in his hand. It was more of a pocket knife than a serious killing knife, but it was sharp and bloody. The blood got my attention because it was mine.

I thought he'd just punched me in the side as I came in, but then I felt the wetness on my side and thought, *Oh gee, he stabbed me with that little blade.* I went to the hospital and got a few stitches.

It wasn't a big deal. Still, I have a deep respect for knives. When I taught self-defense courses, I'd scare the hell out of my students because even as an older guy, I demonstrated that I could get to them with a knife before they could pull their guns.

If a bad guy had a gun, I'd talk to him, because I was confident I could shoot him before he shot me. But if he came at me with a knife, I'd shoot him. A knife is a nasty weapon in the hands of someone who knows how to use it. Most don't understand close-range fighting, but those who do are really dangerous.

I can fight hand-to-hand and I will hurt you because I fight dirty. I fight to win. I will put you in pain like you've never known in your life. I will put you in a wrist lock that hurts so bad you won't be able to breathe. I'll punch you in the throat. I'll break your knee with just eight pounds of pressure. You will limp for many years after and remember me with each step.

I didn't win every fight. I got hurt. It's an occupational hazard, and not one taken lightly, believe me. I wasn't a fan of being beat up, stabbed, or shot at. I would fight to defend myself, but I tried not to shoot at anyone unless a life—mine or someone else's—was in imminent danger.

I was pretty good at defusing situations before guns started blasting. When I arrested someone, I maintained a calm voice. Police always yell, and that is what a bad guy expects you to do, but if you do something he doesn't expect, you get his attention.

My tactic was to hold my badge in my right hand and my gun in left. Then I'd aim at the target's chest and say, "My name is Kenda. I'm with the police department. You are under arrest. If you don't do what I say, I will kill you right here and now."

Even if they had guns, they'd shit because they'd think, *This guy means it!* They would raise their hands without a shot fired. That was my goal. I had no desire to kill anyone.

I probably pulled my gun out twenty thousand times over the years. I could have shot a lot of people, because I usually had the advantage. I might even have received medals for bravery under fire. But taking the advantage to shoot someone makes you just like the bad guys and I'm not like them. I did not behave like that. I had a gun all those years, but I am proud that I never had to kill anyone. I arrested a lot of people but I never injured or shot anybody. It wasn't necessary, and for me, it had to be necessary.

I'm a black-and-white guy. There is no gray. I can make a decision and I will stick with it. I would decide if it was necessary to drop the hammer on a suspect. I kept my emotions in check. Everything slowed down for me in those serious confrontations. I had the ability to calm myself, and that ability proved to be valuable.

I once kicked in a motel room door to catch a former convict who was a very bad guy. I armed myself with a 12-gauge pump shotgun for the occasion. It didn't require marksmanship, just a general sense of direction.

He was in bed when I came through the door. There was a cocked .45 automatic pistol on the bedside table. He sat up when I came in with the shotgun aimed at his chest.

I was six feet away. I didn't say anything. The shotgun said it all.

He looked at his gun. Then he looked at me.

Then he looked at his gun again, so I spoke up.

"My friend, you will not hear this twelve-gauge go off. You will be dead before the sound reaches your ears."

His hands went up. He wasn't frightened. He had been in this situation before. He just realized he couldn't get to his gun before I killed him. I was prepared and I had the correct weapon. He knew I wouldn't miss with double-ought buckshot spraying out of a 12-gauge. Those stainless-steel balls would have taken his head off.

He surrendered, which was the most attractive option he had, by far.

THE RIGHT TO BEAR ARMS

I believe in the right to bear arms, though as a civilian I don't carry a gun and I wish you wouldn't, either, for your safety and the safety of your family. It is your choice. I'm a realist. This is a country born in violence. We became a country by armed revolution. Guns are part of American culture. The American West was expanded by force of arms and it was held and maintained by force of arms when we went to war against Mexico and the British.

We are a warring and ruthless species and nation, no matter what anybody wants to believe to the contrary. We dropped nuclear bombs on civilians not once, but twice. Those who view us from foreign shores are aware of that. They tend to think that if they fuck with us, we will kill them, and it is true.

We have always been that way, though there have been times when we've been less in-your-face about it than others. The recent election put us back in that open, "don't piss us off" confrontational mode. We will always respond to a push with a shove, and maybe an elbow to the throat and a knee to the groin. It's who we are and what we do.

The more intelligent and thoughtful people among us don't feel good about that reality, but here we are. You have to accept things for what they are, and what they are isn't always pleasant.

The United States has a gun culture that will never go away. You can't legislate human behavior in a free society. Our politicians pander to the opponents of gun control in order to survive and hang on to their golden health-care and retirement plans as well as their publicly paid six-figure paychecks even though most of our elected officials couldn't pass the postal exam.

Even if you and I wanted to take guns off the street, there are just too many of them already out there. Making them illegal won't change that. Heroin is illegal and yet anyone yearning for it can find the stuff and buy it in less than an hour.

That said, I could put a stop to dope and guns in a hurry, and so could you if either of us held the job of U.S. president and commander in chief. All we'd have to do is create an American Gestapo, a brutal and secretive police force like the one that terrorized and oppressed those under Hitler's regime.

Go full Gestapo. Do that and all the bad shit goes away. Except the Gestapo, that is. And most of us seem to agree that we prefer our battered and patched democracy to an authoritarian state. We want our freedom. We don't want to be oppressed by dictators and demagogues. We want to live free, and for many people, the right to bear arms is an essential freedom. I'm okay with that most of the time.

I have had hundreds of people threaten my life on a regular basis over the years. I'm still here and I don't feel the need to carry a gun at all times. Even when I carried a gun on the job, I rarely used it unless there was a life being threatened.

BEST SHOTS

People are often surprised when they hear that in all my years in law enforcement, I never shot anyone. It is true, though not because I didn't consider it, or occasionally even try. The closest I came to shooting anyone was in response to someone shooting at me. On one of those occasions, a bad guy with a shotgun took out the windshield of my police cruiser while I was behind the wheel. The glass dispersed his shot and I came out of the car with a cocked hammer on my .357 Smith & Wesson loaded with six rounds.

I was going to shoot him dead because he still had the shotgun in his hands and appeared ready to fire again. Just as I was pulling the trigger, he dropped the shotgun, and somehow—maybe it was the adrenaline, maybe my catlike reflexes—I managed to catch the hammer of my gun with my thumb. I thought the gun had fired, but it hadn't.

After I'd cuffed the guy and put him in the squad car, I opened my gun's chamber and removed the round. It had a crimped cap, which meant the firing pin had just barely touched it before I caught it.

I walked to the back of the squad, opened the door, and handed that bullet to the guy. "Keep this as a reminder of how close you came to dying today," I said. "The next time you think about shooting at a police officer, picture this instead."

He was a dead man if the gun had fired. I was glad it didn't, but for my sake, not his. There were many situations over the years when I would have been fully justified in shooting someone and would have shot them dead if need be because real lawmen are not the Lone Ranger, who always seemed to shoot the bad guys in the shoulder or hand.

Police officers are instructed to never fire our weapons unless we intend to use deadly force. We don't shoot to wing you or to frighten you. We shoot to end your days in this earthly realm.

To aim a weapon at a police officer is to give that officer license to kill you. It is the equivalent of signing your own death warrant. That is always a good thought to keep in mind. I was much slower to fire than most. Don't think that I was too kindhearted. I just didn't feel the need to be hasty, because I was a very good shot and I was fast on the draw. I knew there was no rush, because my first shot would take down the bad guy. I took that very seriously. It was not a game to me.

When I was promoted to sergeant with Colorado Springs PD, I had to leave the detective bureau and do brief tours with the other divisions as a supervisor. On my last night before returning to homicide, I was leading a patrol team on the cocktail shift when dispatch put out a call for three cruisers and my team. It was highly unusual to call out the cavalry like that.

A woman had called in to report that her heavily armed husband had taken a neighbor hostage. She was waiting for us on a street corner. She had an eight-ounce glass of whiskey in hand. No ice. No soda. Just whiskey.

She was a large woman in a muumuu and swaying under the influence. She was just sober enough to still be upright, but barely.

Her opening line to me: "You are going to have to kill him this time."

Intriguing.

"What do you mean by *this time*?" I inquired.

"Before we moved here from L.A., their SWAT team said if he ever did this again they'd kill him."

I reasoned that what was good enough for the City of Angels was good enough for us. I called in our own SWAT team. We seemed to be dealing with a repeat offender who, if the wife was any indication, was likely drunk as well as armed and dangerous.

While we waited for reinforcements, the wife informed me that our guy had a pistol-grip pump-action shotgun. The neighbor who stopped by for a visit somehow upset his host and found himself tied and bound to a kitchen chair. He was holed up in an apartment and watching us from a window.

I got tired of waiting for SWAT and told my guys that I wanted to introduce myself to our friend. I went to the door and knocked loudly.

"Who is it?" he asked.

Like it could be the Tupperware lady?

"You know who it is," I said.

"I have a shotgun," he said.

"Great!" I said. "Let's have a gunfight that is loud and scary, and if you get hit by a bullet there is that hot, searing pain! It makes a guy feel so alive! Or dead!"

Silence.

Apparently, he was one of those people who do not get sarcasm.

"So, what do you think, Mr. Shotgun? Do you want to play? You'd better answer or we are coming in ready or not."

"Wait, I'm coming out, don't shoot."

"Well, all right, come on out!" I replied.

"Don't shoot me!"

"I won't, unless you give us a reason."

The neighbor was still tied to the chair. He'd pissed himself, but I can't say whether it was out of fear or too many drinks prior to being bound.

This one turned out to be easy enough, because the guy was just drunk and stupid and I was able to convince him that I was the crazier of the two of us. It could have gone south in a hurry if we'd come in hot and pumped up for a gun battle. All the younger cops were ready to shoot him, but cooler heads prevailed.

The challenge for police officers is that many of these scenarios are easily resolved even though, at first, they can appear to be volatile. On the other hand, many situations that don't seem like much at first can blow up in a hurry if someone gets overexcited, or stupid.

I took a rookie cop in training with me on a more intense call. The dispatcher had just notified me and this kid jumped in my car. I didn't know him from Adam, but this was a "gunshots fired" call so there wasn't any time to share our life histories.

On the drive there, I did establish that his first name was Don, and that he wasn't exactly a gung-ho, let's-kick-some-ass kind of cop. He seemed nervous as hell.

When we arrived at the scene, an ambulance was parked out front, but they wouldn't make a move until we had cleared it. We made contact with a woman on the front porch. She had a swollen eye and blood running from her mouth. There was a piece of firewood lodged in a front window, half in and half out.

"He beat me up," she said.

"Where is he?" I asked.

"In the backyard."

"Do you want to sign a complaint?"

She nodded yes, so I sent the rookie to my car to get a summons book. I'd had too many domestic violence cases in which the woman called us fearing for her life, but then backed down and changed her story if we took her boyfriend or husband into custody. Once she signed the complaint, I had cause to arrest him.

She signed on the dotted line.

I signaled the rookie to follow me as I headed for the backyard. He looked pale. His color didn't get any better when the woman said, "He has a gun."

She could have opened our conversation with that vital piece of information.

Just then, a voice in the backyard yelled out, "Come back here and get me, you sons of bitches!"

The rookie froze. He seemed to be contemplating a new career path, maybe in animal husbandry. I tried to calm him by being reassuring and supportive.

"Don, if you get killed, can I have your watch?"

"Jesus Christ!" he said.

"Oh good, you are back from the fear zone. Mad at me, but back nonetheless. Now stand here in the front yard and keep this asshole talking while I go around the back way."

While Don engaged our armed and delirious friend in intellectual banter, I stealthed my way around to the back. He didn't see me sneak up behind him, which was a good thing, since he was carrying a Marlin 30-30 deer rifle.

I put my gun to the back of his head.

"Hi!"

He threw his rifle thirty feet in the air. I scared the crap out of him.

"Good, you don't have your rifle anymore, and I still have this gun. Let's have a chat, shall we?"

I called my patrol trainee, Don, and gave him the honor of cuffing his first bad guy. We became friends and even neighbors and he told that story hundreds of times over the years because the experience had helped him overcome his rookie jitters.

HITTING THE TARGET

You can't do your job as a cop unless you control your fears, and you should never aim a gun at anyone if fear has a hold on you. That may not seem make sense, because fear is the reason many people buy guns. My point is that you'll never hit your target if you are shaking with fear. You may not even be aware that you are shaking. You may overcompensate by making the muscles in your shoulders, arms, and hands tense. That doesn't work, either.

You have to be confident and relaxed with a firearm if you are to have any hope of hitting your target, especially if you are shooting at another human being. Even more so if your adversary is a killer criminal with nothing to lose, or anyone intent on causing you bodily harm. I had an elderly retired rancher neighbor who brought over a gun that he'd bought. It was a semiautomatic 9mm pistol. He wanted me to take a look at it.

In the later years of my police career, we moved to a rural area for peace and quiet. He'd been there longer, but there had been reports of break-ins and he wanted to keep a gun in the house. The $700 gun he bought was pretty standard, but it had its quirks, as they all do. I told him that there were a few potential malfunctions with this particular gun that he should be familiar with.

In fact, there are a hundred things that can go wrong with any firearm. I don't recommend buying a gun until you understand potential problems and how to deal with them quickly. I tried to walk him through some of the more common issues, but I could tell he was feeling overwhelmed by the mechanics of it.

I also gave him my standard line of questioning when someone tells me they want to buy a gun for personal protection.

- Are you willing to kill someone with it?
- Do you have training in firing at a human target? At any target?
- Do you know how to do threat assessment for a clear and present danger?
- Do you know how to calm yourself before firing at a moving target?

Again, he struggled with these questions. I could tell that he lacked confidence in his skills with a firearm. Finally, I said, "Do you have a vise in your garage?"

He did.

"Okay then, I'd suggest that you put the gun in a vise, take a good strong file, and file the front sight blade down until the barrel is smooth."

"Why would I do that?" he asked.

"Because that way when some younger, stronger bad guy grabs it away from you and sticks it up your ass, it won't hurt so bad," I said.

He looked at me with fear and disgust. Then he took his new gun and left.

Three days later, he came back to my house.

"I thought about what you said. I went back to the gun shop and returned the pistol, and they gave me back my money."

I told him that he'd made a wise decision.

Before anyone buys a gun, I advise them to honestly assess whether they are capable and truly willing to kill another human being. You don't want to have that inner conversation while there is an armed bad guy standing nearby ready to shoot or stab you, so you should have it at an earlier date.

If you confront a violent person, you will have to be willing to use your weapon to commit a violent act.

The next question, as I told my elderly rancher friend, is whether you are physically capable of using your weapon skillfully. The final insult would be to have a killer use your own weapon against you. If you are not well practiced and prepared, that could easily happen.

The world has an abundance of heartless, cruel, murderous predators who will coldly step up and take advantage of any ineptitude, weakness, or hesitancy you display in their presence. Having a loaded gun in your hands may save your life, but it is not a guarantee, especially if you don't know what the hell you are doing with it.

GUN SAFETY 101

This is something I taught my son and my daughter at a young age, though I have to confess that my original intention wasn't to give them firearms skills so much as it was to scare the hell out of them so they'd never come near my guns at home.

My original plan backfired, so to speak.

Our son, Dan, was about six and our daughter, Kris, was around four years old. They were in the explorer stages, prowling around the house looking for anything that would poison, maim, or otherwise imperil their young lives. This was before gun safes were common. I had guns in the house and I kept at least one of them loaded. I kept them stashed away where our kids could not get at them easily, but kids seem to have radar for finding anything dangerous. I worried that they'd find them one day, which is why I kept my ammunition in a separate place.

I tell people that having guns in the home is a personal choice and a right. I also tell them that on more occasions than I care to count, I've investigated deaths in private homes where the weapon had been introduced into the home to protect the occupants. Too often, it was used to harm them instead.

If you believe possession of weapon will allow you to remain alive during home invasion, but you have children at home, you are faced with a quandary. Where do you keep the gun? If you secure it, then your weapon may not be within reach in an emergency.

My usual advice is "Don't buy a gun unless you are supremely confident that you can use it with great accuracy and protect those you love from it." Unless you have drugs in the house or you live in a neighborhood of drug users and dealers—or some other high-crime area—a gun will likely cause you more trouble than it will prevent. Home invasions that include assaults are rare. Get a good alarm system and go with the odds. It beats waking up to the sound of your five-year-old blasting your weapon at a sibling. Or at you.

Because of my profession, and threats made against me and my family by those I'd arrested, we felt it necessary to keep weapons in the house, yet we had nightmares about our free-ranging kids finding them. Finally, I came up with a plan. I told Kathy we should take our young and restless duo up into the mountains under the guise of teaching them how to shoot and safely handle firearms. I know what you are thinking: They were too young. Kathy and I thought so, too.

You see, my secret goal was to scare the crap out of them by showing them how loud and dangerous guns are. I wanted to instill fear in them so they wouldn't be tempted to even look at a gun until they were old enough to get proper training.

My plan was to first teach them some safety basics, such as always treating a firearm as if it is loaded and never aiming it at another person. Using my best Serious Dad voice, I did my best to portray every firearm as a tool of death and destruction.

"The only purpose of this weapon is to kill a human being. It is not a toy. It is designed to kill and it will kill your mom or me or either one of you, so do not ever go near a gun, let alone pick one up, if your parents are not present. Do you understand!"

They were smart enough to play along and pay attention, but I could see in their eyes that they were way too eager to get their hands around the trigger; even my daughter, maybe especially my daughter. This worried me, but I stuck with the plan.

I first let Dan hold a gun with my hands wrapped around his. I helped him aim at a clay skeet pigeon and squeeze the trigger. Kris was standing right there.

I intentionally did not warn them about how loud it would be. I wanted the noise to scare the shit out of them, and then I wanted to show them how badly the bullet blew up the skeet clays so they'd see the destructive power.

Blam!

I fully expected both of them to pee themselves in fright.

Instead, they were both hopping up and down in excitement.

"Whoa, cool! Can I shoot again, Dad?!"

Oh crap! It did not go as planned. They couldn't get enough of it. Kathy was not amused.

"So, Mr. Wizard, what is your next brilliant idea?"

There was no stopping them after that. That day marked the beginning of many years of weekends spent shooting with the wife and kids in the Arapahoe National Forest. We'd drive up, have a picnic, and then blast away for hours.

We didn't have the money for big family vacations, so this became our main bonding adventure, once or twice a month. Needless to say, our kids became excellent marksmen with pistols and rifles. I taught Kathy to shoot, too, and she can dance a can at fifty yards.

The main focus when they were younger was on target shooting, but when they hit their late teens I gave them instructions on self-defense shooting. The philosophy I shared was that you only present your firearm and point it at someone if you are defending yourself or others from serious bodily harm by an armed adversary.

I taught them to shoot handguns and rifles just with their extended arms, no other support, as they would have to do in a real-life encounter with a serious threat. I taught them about sight picture and indexing. Sight picture is a method for selecting a small portion of the target, like a shirt button, to aim at with the sights on the weapon. Indexing is a shooting technique in which you pretend you are pointing your index finger at the target, but it is the gun. Then, when you pull the trigger, you will put the bullet right where you pointed and drop 'em every time.

They were excellent students. On our first day using human silhouette targets, Kris shot first and put one right through the center of the target.

"My dear, that is a kill shot," I said proudly.

Then Dan stepped up and did the same thing.

It warmed a father's heart.

I taught them there is no such thing as a warning shot. You shoot to kill, not to wound, by taking an extra half second to take careful aim and make it count. They did the body armor drill in which you assume your opponent is wearing a vest so you put two shots in the chest and one in the head.

They learned that if you are going to use a weapon because you believe it is necessary for your survival or the survival of another person, then you should shoot to kill your antagonist right there and right fucking now. When they were growing up, I had a sign in the garage over my workspace: "Due to the increased cost of ammunition, there will no longer be warning shots. Trespassers will be shot and survivors riddled."

THE FAMILY THAT SHOOTS TOGETHER

Needless to say, both my son and daughter became expert marksmen. They were at the top in their military firearms classes. My son and I have continued our gun-totin' tradition in recent years by participating in western or cowboy action shooting competitions. These are target shooting contests and great fun.

In our category, competitors wear period Old West clothing and use replica or original firearms designed prior to 1897. We shoot with Colt Peacemaker Old West .45 single-action revolvers and stagecoach shotguns with 20-inch barrels, and Winchester .45 long Colt lever-action rifles.

What makes it a hoot is that each competitor adopts a cowboy shooter name. My son is Big Dan Doherty. He's a big guy, especially in boots and a cowboy hat. He wears all black and looks like a real badass. I had a sepia-toned poster made of him in his getup, posing with a pistol in each hand.

It says: *Wanted Dead or Alive: Big Dan Doherty. Western Pacific Railroad will pay $5,000 in gold for delivery, dead or alive, of Big Dan Doherty, who was responsible for a train robbery in Roundup, Montana, Sept. 10, 1879. Doherty is a ruthless killer and should not be approached.*

He has that hanging in his office at work. Nobody messes with him.

My cowboy shooting name is Joey Fogerty. I borrowed the last name from my wife's family. People tease me that it sounds like an Irish cowboy who couldn't get a job.

I wear brown cowboy boots and replica nineteenth-century Levi blue jeans with a tightening strap in the back waist because they didn't wear belts then. I have blue or brown suspenders, and I wear a cowboy shirt.

In the summer my cowboy hat is straw. In the winter it's a felt hat with a rattlesnake tail dangling down. My shooting team is called the Colorado Shake Tails and we all wear the rattlers on our hats. I had a leather smith build me a custom two-holster rig for my guns that holds my ammo on the belt. Another craftsman made elk horn grips for my pistol, which are very pretty.

During the events, you approach the shooting line with those weapons while wearing your cowboy clothing, boots, and hat—the whole deal. A range officer stands next to you with a timing device. He says, "Are you ready to shoot this course?"

Before you shoot, you have to recite your favorite line from a cowboy movie. Mine is from the John Wayne 1969 original version of *True Grit,* in which Wayne's character, Rooster Cogburn, is preparing to ride with guns a-blazing against the bad guys and before putting the reins in his teeth says, "Fill your hands, you sons of bitches!"

I know what you are thinking. I never used that line as a detective, though I thought about it now and then.

During competition, you must shoot a pistol target left to right and then right to left. There are time penalties for procedural mistakes. Then you shoot rifle targets in a certain order, and then shotgun targets in a certain order. You fire ten pistol shots, ten rifle shots, and four shotgun rounds.

You are timed and penalized for going over the limits. Technically you are competing for your own best time, but of course, guys are always trying to beat each other's scores. Our goal is to stay in the middle of the time range and to not miss any targets. Some of the competitors are all about winning the $1.50 trophy and they game it by shooting faster with less accuracy, because that's the way to win if you can pull it off fast enough.

They have these cowboy action shooting competitions all over the country and in Europe, too. They are conducted by the Single Action Shooting Society, which issues all members badges with numbers. I wear my badge on my suspenders.

They also have horseback cowboy shooting competitions. You have to be a true horseman, because you ride through a serpentine course, controlling the horse with your knees while you shoot at targets.

Like I said, it's a lot of fun, especially when you run into some of the other competitors in real life. You'll see them at Home Depot or somewhere and say, "Hey, howdy, Pecos Bill!"

People stare at us like we are crazy, and maybe we are, a little.

My daughter doesn't compete with us, but she still target-shoots. She may be the best shot in the family. She scored 100 percent in her military shooting test. Her instructor asked her where she learned to shoot so well.

"My dad's a cop," she said.

No further explanation needed.

My son is a big, strapping guy who holds high military rank, and he naturally commands respect. My daughter will fool you. She's very petite and low-key. People tend to underestimate her, often at their peril. She is small, but mighty and fearless.

As I said, I don't pack a gun as a civilian, but she is a military contractor with high clearance and she keeps a pistol in her purse, which she is not afraid to use if need be. On one occasion, not very long ago, she felt the need.

Kris, who has developed strong spiritual beliefs over the years, believes she was put in this situation by a higher power. I don't know if that was the case, but if it was, that higher power certainly chose the right woman.

She tells the story well. Here is her account in her words:

At the end of a fourteen-hour day, I pulled into a grocery store parking lot. I was still in my work fatigues and combat boots. I was dog tired, but I had a dinner planned and I needed chipotle chili pepper, which is hard to find here in the South.

I thought, *Lord, what am I doing here? I should just go straight home. I am so, so tired.*

The answer I heard in my heart was curious, but clear: "I know, but I need you to pay attention."

I know my Lord's voice, and there is no disobeying Him. I cleared my head, shook off the fatigue, and walked into the store.

I found the chipotle chili pepper more easily than I'd expected. Then, instead of going right to the checkout as planned, I wandered across the store to frozen foods. I had no reason to go to another part of the store, and I can't explain why I found myself there.

Just before I reached the last aisle, I overheard a man's voice saying the most disgusting things of a sexual nature. I rounded the corner and saw him. He was a big guy, about six-foot-three-inches tall, and 250 pounds.

A few feet in front of him was a small woman, whom he'd apparently been making the lewd comments to. Her eyes were wide with fear, and her face was pale and drawn. She had a death grip on her grocery cart.

I walked up to her, making sure to keep him in my line of vision. I'd already put my hand inside my purse, which was in my grocery cart basket. My fingers found the handle of my Glock 26, but I did not draw it out.

"Is this man bothering you?" I asked, using what is known as my no-nonsense "military command voice."

Two things happened next.

The man threw up his hands and quickly backed away, and the woman he'd been bothering blurted out, "Yes! I have no idea who he is. He started following me!"

"Okay," I told her. "He is going away, and we will let him do that. I will stay here with you."

He walked to the end of the aisle and disappeared, but I had no idea whether he'd left the store or remained, or whether he might be waiting for us outside.

I needed her to be calm, so I shifted the conversation tone.

"Are you done shopping?"

She looked at me like I was plum crazy. Then she realized what I was doing. She let out a breath and smiled.

"Yes," she said.

"Good," I said. "I will keep watch while you check out. There's no reason not to do that. Please wait, while I check out right behind you. Then I will get you to your car. You will have to load the groceries yourself, because I need to keep watch with my hands free. Do you understand?"

"Yes," she said. Her tone of voice was even and calm. She was letting me know she could keep it together enough to be an asset, not a liability if things went south.

She told me her name, but I am terrible with names and have since forgotten it. She said her husband was in the air force, like me. They had just moved back to the States with their two small children from Aviano Air Base in Italy.

"Well, welcome home," I said laughing. "You may not believe it right now, but this sort of situation is really unusual for this town."

I didn't tell her what I was thinking. *If I see him again, it will be in the parking lot. And he is going to die. If he comes back after that first encounter, there will be no doubt of his intentions.*

With all of my heart, I did not want any of this to be happening, but it was, and now this lady, who said she had little kids at home, was in my care. All the years of practice shooting in the mountains gave me the confidence to take that responsibility. All the lessons Dad had imparted about staying calm, holding a sight picture, indexing, controlled breathing, and trigger squeeze—all of it was right there for me. Military training came back to me, too, but Dad's voice, reassuring, confident, was the most prominent in my mind.

We scooted to her car. Her antagonist was nowhere to be seen, but I remained on high alert. She opened her car and set a world speed record for loading groceries while I scanned the parking lot around us, with my hand still on the Glock in my purse. She opened her door and thanked me with a warm smile of gratitude.

I watched her drive off and saw no sign of anyone following her.

I unlocked my Jeep, climbed in quickly, and locked the doors. My eyes swept the parking lot again. No sign of him.

I said a prayer of gratitude, thanking my Lord Jesus for my Dad's guidance, and for keeping that disgusting man at bay. I doubt that it occurred to the guy, but he should have been praying in thanks, too. I didn't want to kill him, but if he'd shown his face in the parking lot, he would have died that day.

Two to the chest. One to the head.

TEN

YOU HAVE THE RIGHT TO CONFESS, DIRTBAG

A police interrogation is generally defined as a method for getting a statement from an uncooperative person. If you had a cooperative person, you just interviewed him, no interrogation necessary.

On television cop shows, you hear a lot about the good-cop, bad-cop routine for interrogating suspects. I didn't play that game even with hostile subjects. I needed the person to talk to me. So, I played nice. Now sometimes, for whatever reason, my style or personality wasn't right for the suspect in the room. It happens. In those cases, I stepped aside and let another detective handle the interrogation. There was one detective in particular who could reach people where they lived. He had a knack for figuring out what made the hard cases tick. He'd get inside their heads. It was a gift. I called him in for the most difficult situations because I knew he'd get the information we needed without breaking any rules. He was an important part of our team.

In truth, most humans like to talk. It's our nature, for Americans in particular. That's one of the reasons a high percentage of suspects, about 80 percent, waive their Miranda rights to an attorney and just gab away. You wouldn't think that to be true, but most consider themselves clever enough to get away with lying. They began lying as kids to fool their mothers, so they believe they can lie to the police and walk out the door to freedom. That might have happened once or twice, but not if I could help it.

Sometimes I did run out of clock. There is no exact legal time limit on the length of an interrogation. The Supreme Court has ruled that it must be a "reasonable time." That's generally been interpreted by the courts to mean less than eight hours. The reasoning is that the interrogation shouldn't eat up a whole workday. People need to sleep—even violent, murderous assholes.

I'd keep an interrogation going no more than seven hours, including water and food breaks. Anything longer was pushing my luck with the courts. If I went beyond seven hours and got a statement, the defense lawyer likely could get it thrown out due to "excessive time and pressure."

I took my time, and I rarely screamed and yelled, at least not in the initial phases. I talked to them and let them talk. Once you figure out a person's weaknesses and triggers, you can usually screw with their minds enough to get a confession. I was the good cop and I usually worked alone on interrogations.

I always found that the most effective interrogation tool was politeness. I didn't pull fingernails or beat them with phone books. I killed them with kindness. I rarely raised my voice, unless for dramatic effect. I didn't want them to think I was pissed at them. I tried to establish a rapport, find a middle ground, and open the lines of communication.

I was known for plying them with cigarettes if they were smokers, because it calmed them. I know smoking calmed me back when I was still doing it. We did have a no-smoking sign in the interrogation room and I was well aware of the surgeon general's concerns, but this was the homicide division. The suspect was in the room with me because someone had been killed, and killed recently. I wasn't much concerned about the suspect undergoing slow death from tar, nicotine, and toxins. My goal, if it suited the crime, was to seek justice, which could mean a much quicker death for the guy in the other chair.

My approach to interrogations did vary some. Before I'd sit down with the suspect, I would assess his personality, intelligence level, and emotional state. (I'm using the male pronoun because the vast majority of murderers are male, except when they aren't.) These are the questions I'd ask myself in the first few moments of each interrogation: *Is he capable of conceptual thought? Can he be frightened or is he too stupid to be frightened? Is he likely to ask for a lawyer immediately? Does this person feel justified in murdering the victim?*

That last question is a big one. Most killers do feel justified in murdering their victims. They convince themselves of that, and, more often than not, they believe others will agree with them, if they just pour their hearts out and explain themselves.

I love it when they do that.

INTERROGATING JEKYLL AND HYDE

One of my most exhausting interrogations went six hours and was with a reputedly upstanding young citizen who had a wife and daughter, a good job in his family business, a regular pew in Sunday church, and no criminal record. He did not look like a criminal. He appeared much younger than his twenty-four years, an all-American boy, handsome with red hair and freckles.

This intriguing fellow had managed to present himself to the world as a good guy and straight arrow, but believe me, my friend, he was bat-shit crazy. He was a modern-day Jekyll-Hyde, who had separated the two sides of his double life and shielded the darkest part from the world.

There was no leakage that we ever found. His wife and daughter had not a clue. Neither did his coworkers. They thought he was terrific, a real prince of a guy. He had never kicked puppies, drowned kittens, or knocked down elderly women on the street. I couldn't find so much as a jaywalking charge against him.

No one had any idea of the monster within, except first his victim, and then me, and then the whole world. The case began with the brutal assault of a street prostitute, the most vulnerable of victims.

Yes, they jump into cars with strangers like it's their job. They are in a high-risk business, certainly, but that doesn't give anyone the right to hurt or abuse them. Yet their occupational hazards, which begin with sexually transmitted diseases and drug addiction, often end with beatings, stabbings, shootings, strangulation, and violent death.

This prostitute was in her early twenties and slight of build. Her doctors told me that her young age was the only reason she survived the brutal assault. Victims of vicious attacks have a much better chance of surviving if they are under forty years old. Those older than forty rarely make it. Youth trumps all.

Even so, the survival of his particular victim was remarkable. She nearly took a one-way ride on a dead-end road. Actually, her attacker picked her up and drove her out into the mountains and onto Gold Camp Road, an undulating dirt road in the Pikes Peak area that is well known to hikers and off-roaders. It has long been a hangout for teen parties and ghost hunters prowling abandoned rail tunnels along its path.

Lined by pine trees, the serpentine road is beautiful but treacherous. Now closed to most traffic, it is still used by four-wheel drive and ATV enthusiasts who like the thrills provided by its steep drop-offs, switchbacks, curves, and mountain tunnels. It sprang from a trail created in the 1800s by Gold Rush miners, traders, and stagecoach drivers. Later a rail line was built along it for hauling gold from the mines near Cripple Creek to Colorado Springs.

There were many tales of strange creatures and ghouls prowling the trail and particularly its tunnels. If ever an old dirt road deserved to be haunted, Gold Camp Road was it. The young prostitute's story is now part of the legend. She was lucky she didn't become one of its ghosts.

She was stabbed six times over the course of several hours. Her attacker also raped her and did other unspeakable things. He used a tire jack handle to penetrate both her vagina and her rectum, and he pissed in her mouth. It went on and on.

When he was done torturing her, the madman slashed off a handful of her hair before dragging her out of his truck naked and throwing her off a cliff with a severe grade.

He drove home assuming his victim was dead.

He assumed wrong.

Street prostitutes may be easy to pick up, but they can be not so easy to put down. She was a tough little bird. Her knife wounds weren't fatal. Somehow the blade missed her vital organs and major arteries. Still, she plunged down the severe grade nearly one hundred feet before a clump of dead pines stopped her fall.

Later, we went out and looked at the path of her descent. It was so steep we had to hang on to ropes and step down sideways to stay upright and keep our balance. All the way down to the pile of dead pines, we followed the bloody trail left by the victim as she bounced off rocks and trees in her plunge down the canyon.

In spite of her multiple fractures, along with her knife wounds and all the other injuries inflicted, the assault victim clawed and crawled back up. It took her hours to reach Gold Camp Road. She threw herself over the embankment, staggered onto the dirt path, and collapsed in the headlights of a horrified tourist family in their four-wheel-drive vehicle.

Their mountain trail map had mentioned potential sightings of ghosts, but not live women naked and covered with blood. The tourists were kind enough not to run over her. Instead, they dialed 911. The EMTs and ER team did their jobs. Then I got to do mine.

When I visited her hospital room, she was conscious and in the early stages of pissed off. She displayed a fine eye for important details while describing her assailant and his pickup truck. I came away with enough information to identify him without much trouble.

Once I had a name, I checked him out before we brought him in. His record couldn't have been any cleaner if it had been scrubbed with Bon Ami, Murphy Oil Soap, and a bottle of Clorox. Still, his hardy victim had given us enough to obtain a search warrant.

I rounded up my search team. We went to his perfect home, walked past him and his perfect family, and tore up the joint. This wasn't our first rodeo. We pulled out his bedroom dresser drawers, and taped to the back of one was a handful of the victim's hair.

Gotcha, Mr. Clean!

As careful as he was about keeping his Jekyll life separate from his Hyde life, our suspect couldn't help but collect a souvenir from his sordid and vicious crime. We arrested him and brought him in for questioning. I had enough evidence and eyewitness testimony to charge and probably convict him of kidnapping and attempted murder, but I wanted a confession to seal the deal.

Eyewitness accounts are wonderful to obtain, but all too often they prove to be inaccurate or too vague. Skilled defense attorneys have a thousand ways to tear apart most eyewitness testimony. The more eyewitnesses you round up, the more varied their accounts. Our department's favorite eyewitness was this dope-smoking moron who lived up in the mountains. He was a different breed of cat, a hermit who had no clue that World War II was over.

He just happened to be driving through Colorado Springs and making a pit stop when he witnessed a gun battle that I was assigned to investigate. In the end, he proved to be a pretty good witness, but our initial conversation wasn't encouraging.

"Sir, did you see this shooting?" I asked.

"Yep," he replied. "And I'll tell ya, I been to two hog killin's and a county fair and I ain't never seen nothin' like that!"

That hysterical response became a standard line we'd use whenever we had a strange case or crime scene. It has lived on for many years as our police department's favorite eyewitness testimony, a classic!

I did love a solid eyewitness report, but confessions always were my ultimate goal. I just felt better when I persuaded, or tricked, the bad guys and gals to admit their dirty deeds. It completed me.

The Jekyll-Hyde confession was not an easy one to elicit. The mental walls he'd built around his dark side were thick and strong. His Dr. Jekyll was genuinely shocked that we'd accused him of a crime, and for six long hours, his Mr. Hyde was nowhere to be found.

The upstanding citizen blustered and bawled, rolling through the spectrum from sputtering shock to tears of outrage. How could I have dared to call his pristine character into question? The guy was good—at least the good-guy side of him was good—but every now and then I caught a flash of another side.

About five hours into our little chat, as he once again proclaimed his righteousness and rectitude, I asked a straightforward question that seemed to put a crack in the wall.

"I understand you are sincere when you say you love your wife and daughter, but still you did this violent thing," I said.

"I didn't do what you say!" he shouted.

Even as he maintained his innocence, his eyes went dull and dark, lingering on mine as if he was inviting me, or daring me, to probe further. I'd seen flashes of this lurking darkness over the previous hour. It hit me that he felt justified. He wanted to convince me that he wasn't evil. He was just doing what any man would have done.

Just as I was preparing to bear down, there was a knock on the door of the interrogation room. It was my boss.

I stepped outside.

"Do you see what time it is?" he asked. "You are closing in on six hours."

"Yeah, I'm aware of that," I replied.

"You'd better wrap this up. We have the physical evidence and the victim's identification. We don't need a statement and we don't need to give his attorney any ammunition by squeezing him too long."

The boss wasn't wrong. I still wanted a confession, and I felt like his wall was crumbling.

"Give me a little more time with him," I said. "If I don't get it in the next half hour, I'm done."

My instincts told me that the evil side was pushing to emerge, but the clock was ticking and I'd just about run out of ideas on how to knock down the wall. When I went back in, I fired random questions at him to keep him talking, in hopes of tripping him up.

"What do you like to think about every day?" I said.

"What?"

"Do you think about money? Being a football hero or a movie star? Where does your mind go when it wanders? What are you daydreams like?"

His head tilted sideways at a very odd angle. I hadn't seen him do that before.

"You'll get mad at me if I tell you," he said.

This was a new tone of voice. Deeper and darker.

"No, I won't," I said.

"Oh yeah, you'll get mad."

"No, you can't tell me anything I haven't heard before," I said.

Even now when I think about that moment, the hair stands up on the back of my neck. His whole demeanor had shifted. He straightened his spine. The muscles in his arm flexed and his fingers clenched and unclenched.

Then he really freaked me out, and I don't freak out easily. He reached over with both hands and clasped my hands with his. When he spoke again, the transformation was complete. An entirely different person had stepped into the room. This one was aggressive and arrogant. He was sweating and trembling. The timbre of his voice was conspiratorial and crackling with excitement.

"I like to think about fucking girls in their own blood while they are dying."

Well, all right then.

Welcome to the party, Mr. Hyde, I thought.

The creepy son of a bitch was still clasping my hands in his. I wanted to grab a gun, shove the barrel down his throat, and blast his brains out. That happy thought was dancing in the disco of my mind, but I didn't share my bliss with the deranged man-beast across the table. I held his gaze, and let him hold my hands.

I did scrub them later. Several times.

The tape recorders and video cameras were rolling as his carefully constructed walls came tumbling down, and his dark side emerged. My job at this point was to keep the beast talking and not fuck it up.

"I have to admit, I have thought about doing that, too," I said.

Like we were kindred souls. Just a couple of bloodthirsty, sex-crazed maniacs, sharing our hopes and dreams over coffee and Danish.

"Really?" he said, stepping into my lair.

He then laid out the whole sordid story of his secret life. He'd become obsessed with this perverse dream of having sex with a woman lying in her own blood, and after years of obsessing over it, he'd finally decided to act.

After spilling the story, and obviously enjoying every minute, he capped it off with a lighthearted resolution.

"You know what? Next time I'll make sure she is dead!"

I pulled away from the table and as I stood up I said: "Oh, I believe you, but there won't be a next time. I will make sure of that."

He seemed shocked. I guess he thought we were bloodthirsty bros.

I walked out and fought off a compelling urge to take a long, hot shower to cleanse myself of that crazy fuck, his disgusting touch on my hands, and his entire, evil presence.

I don't have a lot of faith in most attempts to analyze the human psyche. We are such complicated beings. Crazy comes in so many option packages. Still, everything about this guy screamed *schizophrenic*.

He never went to trial, because he truly was out of his gourd. His attorney was afraid we'd go for the death penalty, which was a possibility back then. Even though his victim survived, his vicious attacks qualified him for a death sentence. His attorney had him plead guilty instead. The judge delivered a "creative" sentence, as they say, making sure he'd never be released from prison.

NOT A SCIENCE, AN ART

My Jekyll-Hyde case offers proof that each interrogation is unique. I learned what worked and what didn't work for me and each suspect brought in. I'd make adjustments according to their personalities and demeanors, but not so much because of their sex.

Humans are humans, but women do think differently than men. Women are more dangerous.

Think about it. Who is usually the hunter in nature? Is it the lion or the lioness? She hunts. He eats. Queens rule in the beehive and the ant colony. You don't mess with them. They will tell you what is what and who is who. I had a female suspect believed to have killed her boyfriend's wife. We arrested her. We had not arrested her boyfriend. I had no proof that he was involved, though I had my suspicions that they plotted together to kill the wife so they could live happily ever after on the insurance proceeds. It's a common fairy tale in Murderville.

While I was interrogating the girlfriend, she demanded to know where the boyfriend was. I played dumb.

"I don't know where he is, but I know where he isn't. I know he isn't under arrest like you because you are our only suspect in this murder," I said.

Yes, I was lying, but there were no rules against my lying to a suspect during an interrogation. I was allowed to lie while searching for the truth. I didn't lie to suspects all that often, but it worked in certain situations.

I was known to invent witnesses who'd seen them at the scene of the crime. Of if there were two suspects in custody, we'd keep them separated and I'd tell one of them that the other had already ratted him out. That was fun.

"Yeah, your buddy threw you under the bus a few minutes ago, how about that?"

"What?"

"He told me the stickup was your idea and he was just the driver."

"My idea? It was his idea and he shot the bastard when he wouldn't give up his wallet!"

I loved it when they flipped on each other. There is no honor among thieves. No one wants to go down alone. That's why it is so much fun to be a detective. In the cases of the boyfriend-and-girlfriend murder plot, she wasn't happy that she was arrested and under interrogation while her boyfriend, who had in fact recruited her to kill his wife for him, was still running wild and free.

When I said that we had no reason to suspect his involvement, she decided to set me straight. She took the hook and laid out the whole scenario, saying the boyfriend/husband had planned his wife's murder.

Thank you very much. Now you are both going to prison.

TRUE CONFESSIONS

The girlfriend gave up the truth because she was pissed off at her co-conspirator boyfriend. I pushed the right button—the one that said TALK. Often suspects were not talkative at first, especially the surliest ones. They were always a lot of work, but there were ways to open them up.

I'd use misdirection. Instead of talking about why they were there, I'd ask if they were sports fans. The suspect might grunt yes or no, but usually I could find a common ground and work it. Within an hour or so we'd be swapping our favorite sports stories and talking about our favorite teams like two guys in a bar. Then I'd throw them a pitch that was easy to hit: "You told me why you couldn't have been involved in this, but I can't remember exactly what you said. Could you tell me again?"

You'd be surprised how often a suspect can't remember the alibi given initially. I never forgot. I'd use their own words to trip them up, catching them in lies and fabrications, but always in a nice way. Like a friend in a bar, reminding you that just a few minutes ago you said you were home sleeping and now you say you were watching *Miami Vice*, but you can't remember the plot.

Once I homed in, I was no longer their buddy at the bar. I'd slam my notebook on the tabletop and become Detective Antichrist.

"You're a fucking liar! Oh, you are not lying to me now? Were you lying to me earlier when you had a different story? Exactly when did you lie to me? You fucking liar!"

It's all about timing, and getting their tongues wagging until they talk themselves into trouble. This isn't as hard to do as you might think. Sharing comes naturally to most of us, even the killers among us. The guilty talked because they thought they were smarter than me, which was something I encouraged during interrogations. I wanted them to feel superior, confident, and at ease with the dumbass detective across the table.

They'd also talk because they wanted to be understood and sympathized with. I could be very sympathetic, even with the most bloodthirsty and deranged psychos. Usually they wanted to tell me fantastic tales they'd invented.

I enjoyed the creativity of suspects in the interrogation room. You'd find it striking just how many of them were using the bathroom when shots were fired in the bar. Amazing how often that happened. I'd let them yap and yap until they felt totally in control of the conversation and yapped themselves into a prison sentence.

I avoided confronting them, most of the time. I figured if I kept them talking, they'd end up at the truth sooner or later. So I didn't raise my voice, or use profanity, even though in most cases I wanted to shoot them in the mouth.

My tactic usually was to disarm and distract the suspect. If I walked in and the guy was handcuffed, covered in prison tattoos, and in raging-asshole mode, I knew he was waiting to unload on me at first opportunity.

So I'd ignore him. I'd walk in, throw my notebook on the desk, sit on the floor, roll my shoulders, and do some stretches.

"Have you ever had back problems?" I'd ask. "My back is killing me."

The suspect would be baffled.

What the hell is this cop doing?

I wanted him to be baffled and disarmed by my unexpected disinterest in him and the murder at hand.

After a few minutes of hearing me grunting on the floor, he finally gave in.

"Yeah, I've had back pain for years now," he said.

From there we rolled right along to the finish line.

I may not look like an actor, but I was pretty good at taking on roles, if I do say so myself. I pretended to be a friend to the friend-less suspected killers. I played a not very bright friend, dumb and dumber. I'd walk into the interrogation room, looking disheveled and confused, and say something like, "Looking at this report, I don't know why you are here. Maybe there was some misunder-standing. What the hell did they arrest you for, anyway?"

I'd ask them to write down their stories because I was having a hard time following all the complicated stuff. I'd say it was easier for me to understand if I saw the whole thing in writing.

I'd also work to give them the impression that I believed every-thing they told me. I was good at playing stupid. I know you find that incredibly difficult to believe. Not that some of the smarter ones didn't see through my fake stupidity and just shut up and tell me to go fish. I didn't always get a confession. Sometimes the sus-pects stuck with their lies. On those occasions, I had to stand up and say, "We're done here."

Sometimes I made mistakes, especially in my early days, and especially with cases that made me angry.

A CASE OF PREMATURE ACCUSATION

One of my rookie detective interrogations was a classic screwup. The suspect was brought in after a fatal shooting outside a bar. Our guy had exchanged words and threats with the victim earlier in the night. Then, several hours later, the victim was found shot twice in the chest in the parking lot.

We made our first mistake in bringing this suspect in before we had anything to link him to the murder other than his earlier dispute with the victim. I didn't have many cards to play. I threw out my ace right away.

"We know you had an angry exchange with this guy earlier in the night," I said.

He made no effort to deny that it had occurred just as witnesses had told us. He was up front and he was talking. Instead of keeping him talking, though, I paused for a minute, trying to figure my next move.

The suspect turned the tables and asked me a question: "So what are *you* thinking?" he said.

Like a bonehead, I told him the blunt truth: "I think you killed him."

To which he responded: "I want a lawyer."

If I could have kicked myself in the ass all the way out the room, I would have. Premature accusation has ruined more interrogations than any other cause known to science. If this had been a poker game, the bad guy would have walked away with all the chips. Fortunately, it was a more serious game, and we didn't have to leave the table in shame.

Instead, we ordered up a search warrant, went to his place, and found the murder weapon. He went to prison, and I learned from that screwup. Although some interrogation techniques encourage you to challenge the suspect right away, I found that it never worked for me to be that confrontational. They'd always lawyer up.

I'd go back to my desk disgusted with myself. *You dumbass! You had him talking and then you screwed up by getting in his face.*

There are always interrogation training classes available from police departments, the FBI, and other agencies. They can give you some basics, but you learn what is best for you through trial and error. Every suspect is different. Every interrogator is different. You have to figure out what works and what doesn't in each situation.

I've known cops who had good results by being assholes in the interrogation room, but that wasn't my style. Once I became a supervisor, I let my detectives figure out what worked for them. I didn't get down on them if they blew it, because I also blew plenty of interrogations.

STREET TALK

I mentioned earlier that I rarely used profanity in the interrogation room because my goal was to keep a civil conversation flowing. If I was interviewing hookers, pimps, addicts, hustlers, and the homeless in their natural environments, however, I could be quite fluent in the street vernacular.

It wasn't as though I were Richard Gere trying to act like a homeless guy, but I did drop f-bombs on a regular basis. Profanity is the language of the street. These are people who've been kicked to the curb their whole lives. If you address them in any other way, you become an outsider. They won't talk to you, or they refuse to share information with you if they think you look down on them. You become the enemy. I always found that if I approached them talking in their own language, they were more helpful.

So I wouldn't say, "Excuse me, sir, we were trying to locate a suspect in a crime?"

Rather, I would say, "Hey, we are looking for this fucking guy who pulled this fucking shithead move and killed another doper and stole his stash. Have you seen this motherfucker?"

Another thing about talking to street people: You never really know who you are dealing with. You could be talking to another killer, a drug runner, or someone who doesn't like cops. So you have to practice officer safety techniques. Oh, you've never heard of them? Have you ever noticed when you talk to a patrolman that he stands at least three feet away from you, balanced on both feet in a stance that puts his holstered gun out of your reach?

While you are talking to him, he is taking an assessment, looking at your clothing for any signs of tears, rips, and blood. He checks your arms for needle marks and bruising. He looks at your shoes for scuffs, tears, and traces of blood. The same with your fingernails. And the pupils of your eyes; he checks to see if they are dilated.

When he asks you questions about a suspect he's looking for, he won't say, "How tall was he?" Or "How much did he weigh?" He will say, "Was he taller than you, or shorter?" "Was he heavier than you? Or lighter?"

He might even ask, "Was he younger than you?" but that's often a bigger problem than you might think when dealing with street people. I was always amazed at how many of them had no idea what year they were born.

SHOWING LOVE TO CHILD KILLERS

On a more somber note, I also took a little different tack when doing interrogations during investigations involving the death of a child. The fact is that, as tragic, upsetting, and even as grisly as they can be, most child killings are not intentional. Some are, sure, because there are crazy people out there. The majority, however, are the result of a punishment or discipline effort that went wrong or escalated into violence.

The parent, older sibling, babysitter, or guardian of some kind strikes or pushes or restrains with more force than intended or necessary, and death results. It is still murder, but there was not intent to kill.

These cases are always hard emotionally, but the interrogations are generally not that difficult because these suspects want release from their guilt. They seek understanding and forgiveness even from the cop who wants to lock them up and throw away the key.

Most of those I interrogated for child murder were distressed and emotionally fragile. I didn't play hardball with them. I used a softer approach. Often these suspects had a desire to be forgiven and understood. Once they had those two things, they would spill the beans. That's all I cared about. My goal was to obtain justice for the child and the family.

I didn't really care if the killer had not meant to murder the child. All I cared about was whether the suspect in custody had ended the life of the victim. I wanted to hear that story directly from the perpetrator so I could nail down the case. Sometimes this meant that I had to pretend to be sympathetic to the killer, even if I wanted to strangle him.

I interrogated a twenty-two-year-old military guy whose girlfriend was recently divorced and had an infant about a year old. The couple dated for just a short time before they moved in together. The boyfriend wasn't at all prepared to be a parent.

It's difficult enough if your own infant becomes sick with colic symptoms, which can include sporadic crying and screaming that can go on for hours. There is no proven cure for colic except time. It usually goes away after three or four weeks, but that doesn't make it easy to live with.

The baby's mother worked. One day she left her colicky child in the care of the boyfriend. When the mother came home, she found her baby unresponsive under the blankets. The boyfriend said he had no idea what might have happened.

She called for help. The EMTs and ER staff detected a faint heartbeat initially, but they couldn't save the child. The treating physician found severe bruising all over the face and body. Both of the baby's legs were fractured. The doctor said there was no doubt that this child died from forced physical trauma of an extreme nature.

This was a homicide. We hauled the boyfriend in as soon as we heard the doctor's report. Child abuse makes my blood boil. I had to calm myself before I walked into the interrogation. The suspect was already trembling with fear.

I went slowly. He had denied knowing anything about the boy's injuries, but he knew we were focused on him. He was all but paralyzed with fear and that wasn't helpful for my purposes. I needed to get him over the fear and into remorse. I spent a couple of hours calming him so the remorse could break through. We talked about everything but the murder. I walked him through his own childhood, grade school, high school, and all the things he liked to do growing up.

Slowly, fear loosened its grip on him. I bided my time, and then, when I thought he was becoming more reflective, I calmly stood up, walked behind him, and gently put my hands on his shoulders. Then I leaned down and whispered in his ear.

"I know you are afraid, but you know the truth of what happened to the baby, don't you?"

He didn't say anything. Then he nodded affirmatively.

I walked back to my side of the table and stood in front of him.

"Okay, so you admit you know what happened. Tell me the details."

The details were more horrible than I'd imagined.

He just flat out told me that the child's crying and screaming was driving him crazy, so he grabbed the baby by the ankles and swung him into the wall like a baseball bat.

"He shut up then, so I put him to bed."

If he had called the baby's mother, or 911, doctors might have been able to save the child. Instead he left him slowly dying in his crib for hours. It was a horrible death.

I've had killers tell me things that would make most people throw up, but I'd heard so many of those stories by that time, I just turned into a block of dry ice. That was my chosen method of self-defense. I wanted his confession and I got it. We both had to live with the aftermath.

A CONFESSION IS NOT ENOUGH
FOR A CONVICTION

My interest in obtaining confessions was mostly about seeking closure for the victim's family. I wanted the killer to admit it for them, but I took little joy in it myself, other than feeling like I'd been successful in doing my job.

I did feel a letdown when suspects shut down and lawyered up, as rare as that was for me. Still, I'd chalk it up as a learning experience, and it was. Over the years, I became a better interrogator because I learned from my mistakes. I made sure the detectives who worked for me benefited from my screwups, too. I shared them all, and I never jumped on their asses for making their own mistakes.

Often I'd sit behind the two-way glass and monitor their interrogations. I could usually see when my guys were careening toward disaster, but I'd sit back and let it happen. I never walked in on another detective's interrogation. I always let them continue until the suspect asked for a lawyer, because the bad guy wasn't going anywhere. He was still locked up, and we still had a case based on evidence and witnesses. Or we'd keep working whatever angles we had.

When an interrogation failed, I'd take the officer aside and walk through what had happened. What went wrong? What did you learn? I let them know they weren't in trouble with me. It's never easy. There are no magic steps one through nine to follow for a guaranteed confession. If one of my guys blew an interrogation, I'd tell them there was no harm done as long as they learned something that made them better.

By law, a person cannot be sentenced to prison based on a confession alone. It won't hold up in court if that's all you've got. You could walk into your local courtroom tomorrow morning, raise your right hand, and confess to killing John F. Kennedy on November 22, 1963, in Dallas, but that wouldn't get you thrown in prison.

They might take you to the psych ward for evaluation, but they won't lock you up for murder. They might even investigate to see if there is any evidence to support your confession if you give a convincing performance.

Chances are, they'd do a brief assessment and send you home. It's the same in state and federal courts. You can't go down with just a statement of your guilt. That's a safeguard put in place because there are too many crazy people in the world willing to confess to anything and everything.

OUR SERIAL CONFESSOR

During my detective years, we had an eighty-year-old woman who would read the local newspaper looking for unsolved murders. She'd get the details down and then take the city bus to police headquarters, go to the front desk, and say she wanted to confess to the killing, whatever the murder of the day happened to be.

We had several regular visitors like her. The police are available for everyone 24/7, and if you have access to the phone, we will answer. You call and we haul.

We were particularly fond of this elderly woman. So we'd have her sit down at a word processor and ask her to type out her confession in a complete and thorough statement detailing how she'd accomplished this evil deed. She'd sit stroking the keys for a couple of hours, producing complete gibberish because, along with not being a cold-blooded killer, she was not a very good typist.

Nevertheless, we would let her type away. Our guys brought her a cup of tea now and then to make sure she stayed hydrated. She was a regular—a tiny white-haired person who didn't weigh as much as the big leather purse she always carried. We never checked it for weapons, but she could have kept an arsenal in there. She'd sit it on the floor while typing and it would always fall over.

She'd always come like she was dressed for a party, wearing a nice dress and nylons. In the winter, she'd wear a coat and hat, and she'd never take them off, no matter how warm it was in the office. Once, I asked her if she had family. She said no, she was alone.

It was funny in a way, and sad. She never seemed to mind that we didn't believe her or accept her confessions. I never had the impression that she wanted to be punished or go to prison. She just wanted a day of hanging out with the gang in Homicide. She'd stretch it out, making sure that the last bus had run before she'd get up to leave. She knew we'd have a detective drive her home.

She confessed to murder after murder over the years, probably forty to fifty of them. She claimed to have used knives, guns, hammers, any weapon that fit the descriptions in the newspaper articles. She maintained her guilt until her death. We were sad to see her go.

For a confessed killer, she was a sweetheart.

ELEVEN

MY MURDER TRIALS
AND TRIBULATIONS

My job as a homicide detective was to identify, track down, and file charges against the killer or killers. Bringing them in and charging them didn't guarantee that they'd be found guilty and punished by the judicial system, though.

Many of those I nabbed pleaded guilty, as they should have, and so their cases never went before the court, but 217 of my cases did go to trial. Two hundred fifteen of those proceedings resulted in convictions for those I'd arrested.

Only two of those I identified as killers were set free by the courts.

In the world of sports, most coaches would gladly take a record of 215 wins and 2 losses. Then again, their teams aren't going up against murderers. Coaches don't have to worry that a former opponent might kill innocents.

I tried not to let that bother me, but it did. My job was to make the best possible homicide case and apprehend those I believed had committed the crime. It was the judicial system's job to rule on their guilt or innocence and punish them accordingly.

I was in the *who, what, when,* and *how* business. The judges and juries were in the *why* business. The judicial system made the final ruling. I had to distance myself when I disagreed with their findings. My mental note to the courts was, *You may have let that one go, but I will keep doing my job and find some more.*

I tried to let the losses slide while savoring the victories. I always enjoyed those moments in court when the judge would ask the defendant to rise and then deliver a guilty verdict followed by a sentence that would take a killer off the street for the rest of his or her days.

I liked to think of our criminal justice system as a sleeping tiger. If you go about your life as a good citizen and don't poke the tiger, it will let you pass. But if you are a bad citizen and break the laws set by our society, you will poke the tiger, and it will either take a big bite of you or devour you altogether.

When the tiger let one of my carefully snared catches slip away, I was not happy. One of those cases I am not allowed to discuss. My lawyer has threatened to shoot me if I ever make public statements about it. All I can say is that this was a case in which the alleged killer claimed to have acted in self-defense. I didn't buy that, but the jury disagreed with me.

The other instance in which one of my suspected killers was set free was the trial of a savage multiple killer. This may well be the most disturbing and haunting case of my career. The victims were a pregnant mother and her two little boys. They weren't just murdered, they were tortured brutally. I had never seen that level of violence before and it was very disturbing.

Benjamin Sisneros was an air traffic controller at Fort Carson in January 1979. He had left his wife and children in their apartment early in the morning when he'd headed to work. Around noon, he called home to check in. No one answered. That worried him, so he signed out of work and drove home at 12:10 p.m. It was a thirty-minute drive.

We received a call from him thirty-five minutes later. I was having a slow day until then, looking over cold cases. There was nothing cold about this one, though. When I arrived, Benjamin Sisneros was moaning and crying in deep sobs on the floor in the hallway outside the apartment. He was not the only distraught person present. Our guys, the EMTs, and every other professional responder present was visibly shaken as well. That is a rare sight. This was obviously a horrendous crime scene.

I took a minute to prepare myself, and then I looked in the front door. Inside the humble apartment there had been a massacre; one of the worst I'd ever seen. There was blood sprayed on all four walls and the ceiling. There were blankets over the mother's body, and those of the two-year-old and the four-year-old boys also murdered.

The autopsy would reveal that Yvonne Sisneros, who was three months pregnant, had been stabbed, strangled, and sexually assaulted. That description, as bad as it was, doesn't really cover the extreme level of violence in this case. The killer had rammed a broom handle into her vagina with such force that it stopped at her trachea. The coroner said the injuries from that brutal assault were the cause of her death, not her sixty-three knife wounds.

The children were also brutalized. Their two-year-old boy has been stabbed twenty-two times. The four-year-old was stabbed nineteen times. The killer had used two different instruments to stab them. One appeared to be a cross-point screwdriver and the other was a kitchen knife, according to the coroner.

The killer had beaten both of them before crushing their heads with a weightlifting barbell. A rag had been crammed down the throat of one of the boys. It was so far down, there were fingernail marks found inside his throat.

By the time I walked out of that apartment, I vowed to not sleep until I had the killer by the throat. For such a chaotic murder scene, this one didn't offer up many clues initially. There were no signs of forced entry or robbery. One of the few things that appeared to be out of place was a small writing pen we found on the floor. It was flecked with white paint and blood. I thought it could possibly have been dropped by the killer, so we bagged it as evidence.

When we spoke with Benjamin, he said that when he arrived home to check on his family, he found the door unlocked, which was unusual because his wife was careful about security. Inside he found his wife's body in the bathtub. He was horrified, and without thinking, he pulled her onto the floor and covered her with a blanket. He next found his sons murdered in their bedroom. Then he called us.

The coroner put the time of deaths between 9 a.m. and 11 a.m., a period when the husband was at work. His traffic control work was all recorded, so it was easy to prove that he was on the job at the time of the killings. He appeared to be above suspicion according to everything we had at that point.

I wasn't sure where this case was heading. As often happens, there were some dead ends that sucked up valuable time. We received a call from an anonymous tipster who advised us to check out another resident who lived in a different building in the same apartment complex.

I headed that way with two backup cars. We interviewed a twenty-eight-year-old male, who responded in a normal way and without fear as we questioned him. He had an alibi for the time frame in which the murders occurred. This also appeared to be a dead end.

Standard police work then yielded a much more interesting suspect. One of our officers canvassing the apartment complex and interviewing residents door-to-door talked to a man who'd been walking his dog around 9 a.m. in the parking lot. He'd seen a guy in a plaid shirt and tan pants letting himself into the Sisneroses' apartment.

We learn that this description matched that of "Jimmy," a maintenance man for the apartment complex. This sounded like our first good lead in the case. I homed in on the maintenance man. The director of maintenance for the complex identified him as James Joseph Perry. He added that, as far as he knew, Perry did not have a master key to the apartments.

A quick check revealed that Jimmy did have an extensive criminal record. He had arrived in Colorado after serving fourteen years in a New York State prison for murder. Our background check revealed that he'd started out with small-time burglaries and then more serious sexual assaults of women. His murder conviction in New York State brought a sentence of twenty-five years to life, but he'd convinced his parole board that he'd found religion.

They shipped Perry out when he showed that he'd been accepted to the Nazarene Bible College, in Colorado Springs. There he had gotten into hot water for seducing female students and tape-recording their sex together. He played the tapes for his drinking buddies in a local bar. Word got back to the female students. Complaints were filed.

Based on Perry's criminal history in New York State, his continuing criminal activity on my turf, and his access to the victim's apartment, we had enough to obtain a search warrant. Our first stop was his apartment. When our guys arrived, they met his common-law wife, who had two sons.

She said Perry had been gone all night, probably with one of his many girlfriends.

His disloyalty didn't seem to faze her. She also told our officers that she cleaned apartments in the building where the murders occurred. She had a master key. They asked her to see the key, but she said it was missing.

During a search of the janitor's house, our officers found damp clothes in the washing machine that smelled strongly of bleach. On the clothes were bleached-out spots, indicating a possible attempt to remove bloodstains.

About five hours after we were called to the crime scene, I went to the apartment complex's maintenance office armed with a search warrant. Several other detectives and captains as well as a detective who worked for the district attorney accompanied me. There were about eight of us.

We packed into the small space with the maintenance manager. We told him we were looking for James Perry, as well as any information we could find on him. Our discussion had just started when who should walk in but Mr. Perry himself?

I'm sure the temperature in that office went up about thirty degrees due to all the cop hearts set racing when our chief suspect came within reach. He had a mustache and long curly dark hair. He stood about six foot two and he was muscular from working out in prison, where getting stronger is a survival move, though not always an effective one.

We lobbed a couple of questions about the murders, but Perry didn't know nothin' about nothin'. He was obviously nervous, but then, what lifelong criminal wouldn't be nervous while packed into a small room with sweaty cops?

Tensions escalated when the detective with the district attorney's office observed something that the rest of us had missed: When Jimmy reached for an item on his boss's desk, the detective noticed what appeared to be flecks of blood on the face of Jimmy's cheap watch.

"Hey, Jimmy, is that blood on your watch?" he asked.

Perry nearly melted into a puddle on the floor. We cuffed him and hauled him in for questioning. I was at the head of the list of eager interrogators, but he lawyered up immediately. In the meantime, our guys on the street were hearing that Jimmy's sexual predator ways were well known around the apartment complex and in general.

He'd been accused of molesting and assaulting women. One person told us that Jimmy had been overheard making sexual comments about a woman named Yvonne who lived in his apartment complex.

We had all the evidence we needed to charge him with the three murders and multiple other horrible crimes. We could not charge him with killing the unborn child in the womb of Yvonne Sisneros, because Colorado law says a child must have taken at least one breath on its own, outside the womb, before killing it can be considered murder.

We believed that Perry had planned the attack, taken the master key, waited for Benjamin Sisneros to leave for work, and then entered the apartment. All indications were that he went into a murderous frenzy. He then went home, cleaned up, and went back to work.

FALSE RELIGION

We had physical evidence out the wazoo. The nine-inch screwdriver used to stab the victims was found in Perry's tool belt. He had a key to the apartment. A witness had seen a man matching his description entering the apartment with a key on the morning of the murders. Perry had made lascivious comments about Yvonne Sisneros prior to the killing. I certainly had seen suspects convicted on less proof. He asked for a jury trial and that was his right.

It was the smart decision from his perspective. James Perry committed this crime, I had no doubt. Yet you never know what a jury will focus on. Perry and his attorney played the only cards they had and they played them well.

As you may recall, Jimmy had managed to win early release from prison in New York State, where he'd been sentenced to a term of twenty-five years to life for murder. He'd told the parole board that he'd gotten religion and was accepted for enrollment in Nazarene Bible College in Colorado Springs. The parole board, probably eager to save the cost of holding him until he died, set him free.

Perry, who never knew a sin he didn't commit, figured God saved him once, and so maybe God would save him again. He used the same ploy during his trial. His attorney selected jurors from the city's large base of evangelical Christians, and he played to their sympathies during the trial.

The defense lawyer even made the risky move of asking his client to take the witness stand. This can be dangerous, because once the accused is on the witness stand, he can be cross-examined by the prosecution. Perry and his lawyer were willing to take that risk and it paid off.

Perry played the God card, saying that after a wayward life, he'd found faith in prison and given his life to the Almighty. He said being a Christian changed him for the better, and he had moved to Colorado to start a new life. Perry swore on the witness stand that with God as his witness he did not kill Yvonne Sisneros and her sons.

To my shock and horror, and to that of everyone else familiar with the facts of the case, the jury bought it.

James Perry committed one of the most brutal multiple murders I've ever investigated and he walked out of the courtroom laughing at me. A lady from the jury came up to me after the trial, which wasn't good timing on her part.

"I think you are probably pretty upset with me," she said.

"I don't get upset, I'm a professional," I responded. "I told you what he did to that poor woman and her children. That's my job and I did it."

"Well, he wouldn't have invoked the name of our Lord if he was responsible for that," she said.

"Maybe that is your Lord, but it's not mine," I replied. "Let me explain something else to you. When James Perry comes crawling into your window and abducts you and your kids, that won't upset me, either, because I'm a professional."

She went home to mull that over. I went home and hugged my wife and kids for a couple of hours.

As an aside, another woman on that jury was a friend of my wife's. Their friendship was never really the same after that, and it ended totally sometime later when the woman asked if I would help her son with criminal charges he was facing. I refused, not because of the Perry case, but because I never played that game.

If we'd had DNA testing back then, the outcome would have been different, because we had plenty of samples on Perry's watch and other items. The mountain of evidence we had against him included testimony from several people who saw Perry shadowboxing after a few drinks and heard him say, "Oh man, I can handle three people at once."

Especially if they included a defenseless pregnant woman and her two tiny boys.

I thought we had enough to convince the jury anyway, but apparently not. Jimmy the janitor's Christian conversion was more convincing to this jury, it seemed.

JUSTICE DELAYED, BUT DELIVERED

I've heard it said that the Lord works in strange ways, and if that's true, this case offers evidence to support it. Less than a year after Perry walked out of the courtroom, a detective from the New York City Police Department's Brooklyn division called me at my desk. He asked if it was true that James Perry had walked on three murder charges in our jurisdiction. I confirmed it as true.

The NYPD detective then told me that after the not-guilty ruling in Colorado, Perry had returned to his Brooklyn birthplace, which also had become his final stop in a long life of crime.

"Perry jumped or was thrown from the tenth story of a Brooklyn building last night," the detective said. "He died of cement poisoning. His case has been ordered to a higher court."

"Yes, that would appear to be true," I said. "Hopefully he's appearing before his final judge as we speak."

The Brooklyn cops later sent me a Polaroid photo of Perry's body on the sidewalk. He looked like a No. 10 can of tomatoes that had exploded on the pavement. I kept that photograph in my desk for seven years. Whenever I was having a bad day, I'd pull it out, look at dead Jimmy, and feel better. His death proved that justice can exist in our world.

As far as I know, there was never any determination of just how Perry happened to take a dive off the building. The Brooklyn detective said they filed his murder case under "Had It Coming."

My guess is that, given his many crimes and many enemies, nobody really cared to delve too deeply into that mystery. I sure didn't, even though I'm known to enjoy a good mystery now and then.

The system of justice in our country is based on the accused having a presumption of innocence. I'm told that the founders of our country had fled England, where those charged with a crime were considered guilty by the state until they proved their innocence to the court. Our founding fathers thought that was unfair, so they wrote the presumption of innocence into our laws, making it the state's responsibility to prove guilt.

Our laws offer the options of a trial by jury of our peers, or a trial by judge. If you are ever dragged into our justice system for a crime that you did, in fact, commit, you should follow James Perry's example and ask for a trial by jury.

If you did not commit the crime that you are charged with, your best bet is to go before a judge if you have facts to support your innocence. Juries can tend to make rulings based on their emotions, beliefs, and prejudices. Judges will usually make their rulings based on the law and the evidence presented.

If you have nothing to lose, I'd suggest you go with the jury trial, but know that it could go either way. Jurors might vote to convict your ass because they don't like your race or your haircut. Or they might set you free because you remind them of their favorite nephew.

You didn't ask, but I'll add anyway (it is *my* book, after all) that I am not an advocate of the death penalty, because I don't have all that much faith in our justice system getting it right. I've seen too many examples of the right guy walking and the wrong guy being sent to death row. I simply don't trust juries.

If you think juries are finders of fact in trials, you are mistaken. They are everyday people, not trained professionals. Like most people, they often make decisions based on personal experience, prejudices, and the fact that the sweater they are wearing is making them overheated and itchy. Many and varied factors come into play, not just the simple facts of the case.

The American justice system is designed to protect the innocent and to reduce opportunities for draconian and ruthless punishment even of the guilty. The design of our system is well intentioned, and it allows room for errors. Sometimes people who didn't do anything wrong go to prison. Sometimes bloodthirsty killers like James Perry walk out the door to freedom.

The infamous Casey Anthony case is another one that many consider to be a miscarriage of justice. This twenty-year-old single mother in Orlando, Florida, was charged with the death of her two-year-old daughter. The daughter was last seen on June 16, 2008. Her grandmother reported her missing July 15 of that same year.

Casey Anthony initially claimed her daughter vanished after she left her with a babysitter, who also had disappeared. That story didn't sit right with detectives. When they searched the mother's car, their cadaver dog picked up the scent of human decomposition. Air samples confirmed the same finding.

Following a grand jury indictment for murder and other charges against Casey Anthony in October 2008, she pleaded not guilty. Her daughter's remains were found by a utility worker about two months later in a wooded area near the Anthony home. Prosecutors announced they'd seek the death penalty.

The trial lasted about a month and a half. Casey Anthony did not testify. The jury deliberated nearly eleven hours and came back with a verdict of not guilty on charges of first-degree murder, aggravated child abuse, and aggravated manslaughter of a child. They did find her guilty of four misdemeanors, for providing false information to law enforcement. Anthony was sentenced to four years on each count, but given credit for time served during the investigation and trial. An appeals court later reduced it to two counts. She served only about ten more days after the trial.

In my opinion, the jury saw Casey Anthony as a confused single mother. They weren't about to send her to her death with a guilty finding. They didn't want to kill her, so they let her walk. That happens when you have a jury trial and the burden of proof is on the state.

I've been asked my opinion of Anthony's guilt or innocence many times, but I'm not comfortable offering it without a thorough review of the case file. I won't offer an opinion based solely on the press coverage. My stance is, "Don't tell me what you think, don't tell me what you believe, just tell me what you can prove. If you can't prove it I don't care what you think or what you believe."

I will tell anyone, however, that there is no system of justice I would choose over ours. It's not a perfect world. We don't have a perfect system. Yet, as imperfect as it is, I don't see anything better out there. For all of its weaknesses and all of the mistakes that happen, our rate of success is still better than most. I accept it for what it is, imperfections and all.

Many of the jurors in the James Perry trial had second thoughts about their not-guilty ruling. They refused to do interviews and asked that their names be concealed in public records. From my viewpoint, they had every reason to be embarrassed, and I wasn't alone. There was such a public outcry that it triggered a ballot initiative to eliminate the trial-by-jury option in Colorado. That effort ultimately failed.

This was an extreme example of a jury that was bamboozled by a defendant, but there are many others, and I'm sure there will be even more in the future.

COURTROOM STRATEGIES

My approach to testifying in my homicide cases was to stick with the absolute truth as I knew it. I never embellished the facts. I remained unemotional on the stand. The one thing I did, purposely, to annoy members of the defense bar was to never respond directly to them when they questioned me.

I always looked at the jury as I spoke. They were my audience. I made eye contact with each and every one of them. This drove defense attorneys crazy. The defense lawyers didn't want the jury to trust my testimony. They wanted them to daydream or nap when I took the stand. I looked directly at each juror. I talked to them to make sure they paid attention.

I've seen jurors nod off in court many times. This is most likely to happen when an expert witness is called. They tend to be very professorial. By that, I mean boring know-it-alls. A paint company chemist testified as an expert witness in the Perry case about some paint flecks found on Perry's watch and clothing that matched paint samples taken from the Sisneros apartment.

I got the feeling the chemist didn't get out much. He appeared to be in his glory. He regaled the courtroom with his vast knowledge of paint and its chemical composition. He had a slide show. By the time he was done, we all could have gone home and made our own interior latex paint in the garage—if we'd stayed awake. Some of us definitely snoozed. The judge had to ask a bailiff to wake up a couple of jurors in dreamland.

The paint wizard continued on for hours in a droning voice. Listening to his expert testimony was like watching paint dry.

As I said, my tactic of talking directly to jurors to keep them engaged, or at least awake, aggravated the crap out of the lawyers for the accused. They would become so pissed off they'd ask the judge to order me to look at them and not the jury. Judges usually took my side.

Veteran defense attorneys didn't mess with me, but occasionally I would chew up and spit out rookies or out-of-town lawyers. After a few minutes of my testimony, they'd be begging me to leave the witness stand as quickly as possible. Every now and then a new gun would ride into town and think he could trip me up. It usually didn't go well for him.

This happened in a case involving a murder in a retail store. The young defense attorney thought he was clever. In my testimony, I said I'd found the thumbprint of the bad guy under the coin tray of the cash register. This is fairly common.

Robbers look under the coin tray because they know merchants put large bills there. Detectives and crime scene investigators also know this, and we know the robbers know, so we look for fingerprints there.

The young defense lawyer homed in on this part of my testimony. He ranted on about the fact that the defendant was a regular in this store, so finding his prints inside it didn't mean he'd been the killer in this case.

I let him babble on.

Finally, I said, "It's true that he'd been in the store many times, but very few customers are allowed to make their own change."

The distinguished members of the jury cracked up. The judge did, too.

Mr. Clever for the defense looked like he'd been strangled. His client went down for the murder. The rash young lawyer and I eventually became friends and often had lunch together. He admitted that I taught him a lesson. He never again tried to wing it with me on the witness stand.

DISORDER IN THE COURT

Judges are very serious about maintaining courtroom decorum. It is called law and *order,* after all. They don't hesitate to pound their gavels if someone disrupts the proceedings, and I've seen judges ship witnesses, spectators, and even attorneys off to jail if they refused to follow the rules.

There are times, though, when the craziness of the world and its occupants leaks into the courtroom. Since the typical trial atmosphere is often tense and very formal, when things go awry, it is all the more startling, and sometimes even hilarious. Lawyers can be every bit as strange as the general population. They can buckle under pressure and lose it altogether.

During a murder trial involving a love triangle, this odd-duck district attorney seemed to lose his train of thought while questioning me on the stand. Or maybe I derailed him by actually giving him straight answers. At one point, he just zoned out and stared into space like his brain had blanked out.

Finally, he looked at me and said, "Sergeant Kenda, what was your state of mind when you arrested the defendant?"

This just isn't a question that a prosecuting attorney asks of a detective. Our state of mind has nothing to do with anything. As Joe Friday said, "Just the facts."

The district attorney and the detective work together on cases.

We are on the same side for the most part. So this question raised eyebrows all over the courtroom. In fact, the defendant's attorney was so outraged by such a stupid question that he threw his pencil down on the tabletop. It bounced so hard that it flew up and stuck in the ceiling panel over his head. The next time I'm in Colorado Springs, I should check to see if it is still up there.

The sight of the pencil in the tile above the defense table set off a snickering epidemic in the courtroom, which is like laughing in church. For some reason, even adults in a serious setting like a criminal trial sometimes find themselves unable to control laughter.

Courtroom circuses are usually set off by incompetent performances by the lawyers involved, or crazy antics from witnesses. Occasionally you get both. One of the most memorable examples of this in my career occurred during a sentencing hearing for a murderer. It's common in these hearings for defense attorneys to bring in character witnesses who testify that the convicted killer really is not that bad a person. He just had a tough childhood. Or the killing was a blip in an otherwise gentle life.

Usually the character witnesses are clergymen, coaches, politicians, or former employers. In this case, the defense attorney must have had a hard time finding anyone from those realms of life to come to court and say the murderer was really a prince most of the time. Instead they brought in a guy wearing bright orange coveralls with COUNTY JAIL stitched on the back. He was in handcuffs and a belly chain that led to leg irons, shackles that are usually reserved for inmates prone to violence and flight. So it was clear that he wasn't a prince himself.

Most of us seated in the courtroom started to snicker and roll our eyes as soon as this character witness shuffled in, but we lost it when the judge asked for his name and place of residence. The star witnesses put his head down and mumbled: "My name is Rufus Washington," he said. "I reside in the El Paso County Jail."

The judge, who was fighting to keep his composure, looked at the defense attorney and said, "This is your character witness?"

The courtroom went up for grabs at that. I looked around, wondering if this was a *Candid Camera* episode in the making. More than a few people questioned the defense attorney's credentials, or they at least wondered what he'd been smoking when he decided to haul a convict out of jail to serve as a character witness. Who needs friends like that?

That thought ran through my mind as I hid behind a case file, trying not to bust a gut laughing in another moment of courtroom hijinks. This too, was a murder trial and serious business. As the prosecution was laying out a very strong case against a very bad man, one of the defendant's buddies in the spectator gallery lost control of his mind.

He stood up and shouted, "This is bullshit!"

The judge responded sternly, as they tend to do, by unleashing the two deputies in the courtroom with an order to subdue the belligerent spectator and take him to jail for thirty days.

While being handcuffed, the stand-up guy glared at the judge and shouted, "Fuck you, man."

"Make that sixty days in the county jail," replied the judge.

"I don't give a fuck," retorted the disruptor.

"Ninety days!" said the judge. "Any further remarks, sir?"

Silence.

Apparently, ninety days was his ceiling for giving a fuck.

You don't see television and movie cops spending hours and hours in courtrooms as they wait to testify, or testify, or stand around waiting for verdicts, but that is a big part of a homicide detective's job. I spent many hours in courtrooms, too many.

Yet, whenever I was called to serve jury duty, I saw it as a civic responsibility and I'd show up on the appointed day like a good citizen. I'd take a seat in the jury selection room with hundreds of other people who were annoyed about having to take time away from work and other responsibilities.

They didn't appreciate the fact that the state of Colorado, unlike most states, has a one-day, one-jury maximum. You show up at 8 a.m., join the jury pool, and if you are not selected to serve on the jury for a trial that day, you can go home and resume your normal life. Many other states keep you hanging around for days in the jury pool.

Now, the chances of a defense lawyer allowing a homicide detective to sit on the jury are slim to none, but I was game if they were. They weren't, and neither were most judges. Usually they don't pay much attention during jury selection. They sit in their chairs on the bench, but they do paperwork while the attorneys interview jurors during the selection process.

On occasion, though, a judge would look over, probably checking out the jury for any known criminals, family members, or attractive women, and see my familiar mug. More than once, I had a judge spy me and interrupt the proceedings.

"Detective Kenda, what are you doing in my jury box?"

"Your Honor, I was called to serve and I reported to duty like a good citizen," I would respond.

The usual judicial response was "Detective Kenda, get out of my courtroom. I see enough of you."

The few defense lawyers who did not know me were shocked that I'd even showed up. Those who did know me usually enjoyed seeing me banished.

Once I did get pretty far along in the jury selection for a civil trial. Attorneys and judges were more likely to allow my presence for a civil trial. This one was a paternity suit. I was surprised when both lawyers accepted me, but the judge wasn't having it. This was before the days of DNA testing. I had established a reputation as being very knowledgeable about blood types, which can play a big role in paternity cases.

The judge looked at me and said, "Kenda, are you not often called to testify as an expert on human blood components in court cases?"

"Yes, Your Honor, that is true," I said.

"You are dismissed from this jury. Please go back to work catching killers," said the judge.

Hey, I tried to do my civic duty, but I never argue with a judge.

COLD CASES

As I noted at the beginning of this chapter, I only lost two court cases in my career, and even though one of those killers ended up splattered on a Brooklyn sidewalk, I still don't like having those losses on my career scorecard. Like most detectives, I also had murder cases that I just couldn't crack for one reason or another. They bother me, too.

Upon my retirement, I had thirty-one cold case files for murders I had not solved.

I'm grateful that one of them was resolved in 2014 thanks to DNA testing, which wasn't available when I worked that case. Police departments keep cold cases open for this reason and others. The science of investigation advances, alibis rot away, or guilt sets in for either the killer or someone who had protected him.

In this case, the detectives in my former department were looking at old cases and realized that the file still contained samples that could be tested thanks to recent advances in DNA testing. The killing involved a girl who was raped and murdered by her mother's boyfriend and a companion. Her body was found on a mountainside.

I had suspected that the mother's boyfriend and his buddy were involved, but one of them was murdered in Mexico before I could prove it. My other suspect thought he'd escaped arrest, too, but his DNA brought him down after the detectives jumped on his cold case and warmed it up.

Of the thirty remaining cold cases with my name on them, I

identified strong suspects in sixteen of them, but was never able to gather enough evidence for an arrest and conviction. In fourteen of the cold cases I left behind, well, I don't have a clue who the killer was, other than it was somebody on the planet Earth.

I torture myself over these unsolved murders even today. It's like reading a book all the way through and then finding there is no conclusion to the story. No closure. The end never comes. It's damned frustrating. There were many times when I'd sit up in bed in the middle of the night because a cold case was driving me crazy. I'd jump out of bed and start making notes on a pad I kept nearby.

I've always felt that I owed it to the victims and their families to find the killer. Still, no matter how much I wanted to solve them, no matter how hard I tried, no matter what I did, there were some I couldn't solve.

It's not that the perpetrator is a genius or a master of deception. It can be for a lot of reasons: In some of my cold cases, no one saw the killer at the scene. In others, the victims had so many enemies that the suspect list was endless. I once had a murder case in which the victim was a drug dealer who was universally despised. At least one hundred people had threatened to kill him at one time or another—sometimes at the same time. He screwed so many people on drug deals, he might as well have walked around with a sign around his neck saying, "Murder me!"

It took me three years to resolve that case because his enemies list was longer than Nixon's. It was one of the few cases I've had in which most of the suspects I interviewed said, "Look, I wish I'd killed that bastard, but I never got around to it."

LUCK RUNS BOTH WAYS

Some cases never got resolved because the killer was just lucky. He left no clues. He lived with the victim, so fingerprints and DNA meant nothing. He had an alibi that could not be broken. Luck comes into play if there is no trace of evidence, nobody sees the killer at the scene, and the body isn't discovered for a long period.

Then again, luck can run in the opposite direction. I had a case in which a murder occurred in a residential neighborhood during the day, but the victim wasn't discovered for several days. As a result, the killer had a long time to get away even before we knew a crime had been committed.

Usually this makes it tough to gather evidence and track down the bad guy. We had no clues, so we began the routine police work: canvassing the neighborhood. Most of the time, no one had seen anything. If they had, they'd have called us at the time. Every now and then, however, Lady Luck was on our side.

During the door-to-door interviews, we found a sixty-eight-year-old woman who'd had a minor stroke. Normally you would not expect such a person to be a good witness. She wasn't. She was a freaking great witness.

Her physical therapist and doctor had her on a program that included mind and memory exercises. Part of her therapy was to sit and look out her front window each morning and take notes on events in the neighborhood. Most days it was pretty routine stuff. The mailman comes by. A delivery truck. The paperboy.

Our detective asked the woman if she had her notes from the day of the murder. Of course, she did. She produced her ledger book. She knew the killer, so she wrote down his name, a description of the car he was driving, its license plate number, and the time of his departure.

The detective came back into our office with the ledger book. He put it on my desk and said, "You're not going to believe this."

He was so excited, he could barely talk.

I was shocked. We don't usually get that lucky, but there was another case I can recall in which fortune smiled upon the Colorado Springs homicide division.

These days, electronic surveillance has advanced beyond anything available in the 1970s, '80s, and early '90s when I was on the job. Back then, the few surveillance cameras that worked in banks and convenient stores usually had really poor-quality video. They also tended to use the same videotapes over and over, which didn't help. Even if they captured a crime, it was hard to make an identification of the bad guys. Most of the time we were lucky if we could tell what sex and race they were.

We didn't get our hopes up when the Asian owner of a liquor store in a bad part of town told us he had a video recording of an armed robbery that he was lucky to survive. He was alone, running his store when a guy came in with a gun. As the owner was cleaning out the cash register for him, the robber kept turning his head to watch the front door.

The ballsy store owner noticed this and waited for his opportunity. When the bad guy turned his head again, the owner smashed him in the face with a full whiskey bottle. The robber went down, but he got back up. He could hardly see because of the cuts and swelling in his face, not to mention the whiskey burning in his wounds, but he grabbed his pistol and shot up the place, emptying his gun.

The store owner somehow managed to dodge the bullets. The nearly blinded robber ran out and escaped. I was heading up the assault unit then as part of my supervisor training to become chief of detectives.

My guys went to the store and interviewed the owner, who said he had the whole crime on videotape. As I noted, we usually found this to very poor-quality footage and not much help to our investigation. This case was different.

This owner was an electronics buff. His store was in a high-crime area. He cared about his employees more than most. He had invested in top-of-the-line surveillance gear from a German company, and he had it properly installed.

When our guys looked at the footage of the armed robbery, they said, "Holy shit, this is like watching a real movie." It even had surround sound, or at least very good sound.

Based on the video, we identified a suspect with a history of armed robbery who looked very much like the robber in the video. We couldn't find the guy right away, but we brought his mother in to look at the video.

I told her that there was gunfire, but no one was hit, and that she might be distressed because she might possibly recognize the shooter. She was a churchgoing woman, and she was ashamed that her son was a known criminal, so I thought she might be cooperative.

When we played the video for her, she studied the robber and started crying. She watched the whole thing and, at the end, said, "That's my son. Oh my God, is he all right?"

He didn't live with her anymore and she hadn't seen him in a while. She gave us the last address she had for her son. I sent two guys to arrest him. They came back with hangdog faces.

"We found him—in jail. He's been locked up there for four months."

That made for a fairly solid alibi.

His mother had fingered the son without knowing he was behind bars. She had honestly thought it was him. As it turned out, we later caught the real robber, and he could have been the son's twin. They looked very much alike, except the real robber had some nasty scars from being slammed in the face with a full whiskey bottle.

Often cases go cold because the killer has an alibi provided by friends or family members. They live in fear of the murderer. They love him and provide an unbreakable alibi. Until they don't.

TOO MANY SUSPECTS

I had one case that went cold for nine years before we solved it. This was a difficult investigation because the victim had a long criminal history and more enemies than friends. He lived in the city's crime-infested underworld, where everyone is a predator and nobody knows nothing.

The victim had been hit by a car when he was eight years old and it left him locked in that mental age for the rest of his life. As an adult, he worked for Goodwill Industries in a community program for the disabled. He lived in a fleabag residential motel infested with drug addicts, alcoholics, thieves, hookers, and pimps. It was such a pit that the most upstanding residents were the cockroaches and rats. This was not the Ritz-Carlton. Maybe the *Shits*-Carlton.

You get the sordid picture. It was not a healthy environment for anyone, but especially the victim. His mental challenges included an impaired ability to assess the characters of people around him. He trusted dirtbags who took advantage of him by stealing his money, drinking his whiskey, eating his food, and blaming him for crimes they committed. He was arrested many times for minor crimes but was never convicted because he was always taking the rap for others.

His one decent possession was a cheap radio, worth maybe forty dollars. Someone entered his place while he was home, stabbed him thirty-one times, and stole his radio. Cheap radio. Cheap life. That seemed to be the attitude of those who knew him. Nobody cared.

I cared. The victim's criminal record or moral character never mattered to me. This person's life was taken. I wanted the killer. I worked his case as if each victim were the most important son of a bitch on the planet.

In this case, none of his neighbors or so-called friends cooperated. Most of them were among the fifty-two suspects I identified. While I was working this case, a new detective came on board. I asked him to help me. His response was "Is that the guy from the West Side motel? Who cares about him?"

That was the wrong thing to say to me. The other detectives in the room turned away because they knew I was about to go ballistic on the new guy. Their first clue was when I turned red, then white with rage.

"Don't you ever say that to me about any human death on our watch," I said. "If you ever do, I swear you will be writing parking tickets at the airport from midnight to eight with Tuesdays and Thursdays off for the rest of your career! Is that clear?"

He got the message. I made sure he worked his ass off on the case, but it still took me nine years to solve it, and we had some strange developments along the way.

Five years into that investigation, a Colorado state trooper picked up a hitchhiker outside Colorado Springs. While the trooper was checking his identification, the guy blurted out, totally out of the blue, "I killed that guy on the West Side five years ago."

We were ecstatic, for about five minutes. The hitchhiker turned out to be a lunatic. He had nothing to do with the killing.

Over the years, we kept the case open, hoping for a break. While we waited, DNA science advanced, and one of my crime scene observations paid off. We'd found blood drops at the scene that appeared to be those of the killer, who'd cut himself while stabbing the victim and then washed off in the apartment's sink.

His blood had dropped on the floor around the sink in a splatter pattern characteristic of blood dripping from an open incision. I saw the droplets of blood and thought, *Our killer cut himself.*

I'd recovered some of the blood and preserved it as evidence in case. The sample from the prime suspect also led us to his accomplice. Both of them went down. This was the case I mentioned earlier in the book—the first Colorado murder conviction won with DNA evidence.

Every now and then, time works on your side. Relationships change. Guilt grows. That is why we keep cold cases open. For the same reason, the killers I didn't catch should sleep with one eye open and a packed bag by the back door. Another generation of detectives is still hunting you. And I'm still around to help them do that.

To all those killers I haven't caught, I hope you aren't sleeping well. I hope life has not been easy or good for you. And I want you to know, I have not forgotten you. Neither have the detectives who regularly review cold cases. The homicide file with your name in it is active. Cold does not mean closed.

PART IV

RETIREMENT AND RECOVERY

TWELVE

HONEY, I'M HOME, DON'T MIND THE BLOOD

was in my unmarked car with another detective, looking for a homicide suspect in one of the worst parts of town. A call came over the radio: shots fired at a residence.

The dispatcher gave the address and, strangely enough, we were right there.

We parked and ran to the front door of a dump of a house.

We could hear screams. We drew our guns and kicked the door in.

"Police!"

In the kitchen, we found this fucking guy in a one-inch puddle of blood growing deeper and wider by the second. The blood was pouring out of the hole in his face. His wife and kids had found him and called 911.

He'd shot himself with a stainless-steel Smith & Wesson .357 Magnum. That should have done the job. He had the right gun, but the wrong aim. He had pointed the barrel at the temple of his forehead, and as he pulled the trigger, he flinched.

That happens sometimes, and the results are never good. He blew off his eyes and his nose, but he was still alive.

His suicide still might have been accomplished if we hadn't been right on top of his house. Blinded, he was on his hands and knees in the puddle of blood, feeling around for his gun on the floor so he could finish the job. We dove on him and wrestled away the gun, slipping and sliding in the gore.

Once we had him pinned, I shoved a kitchen towel into the gaping wound and compressed it as best I could. He wouldn't have lasted long, because the blood was still pouring out of him, but the EMTs blew in right behind us, wrapped him up, and rushed him to the hospital.

He would survive, for better or worse. We searched the house for any other possible victims. The wife and kids were okay, but the place was such a shithole that we called child protective services. The only toilet in the house was backed up, so they'd been using the bathtub instead. We also found a container in the kitchen that was so vile I had it bagged and taken to the lab out of fear that it was toxic waste. It turned out to be three-year-old macaroni and cheese.

Darkness had set in before we got out of there. In the streetlight I looked at the other detective and, for the first time, noticed that he was still drenched in blood.

"If I look anything like you, we are a mess," I said.

"Oh, you do," he said. "And we are."

That is why I never paid more than a hundred dollars for a suit. I had a guy who worked in the men's department at a very nice store in the mall. He basically dressed me. He called me whenever they had a sale to clear the racks for a change in seasons. Every six months I'd pay $500 or $600 for three or four suits, including shirts and ties to match that he picked out for me.

Because I got my work clothes so cheap, I didn't feel bad when I had to throw them away. No dry cleaner would accept them soaked in blood.

That night I dropped the other detective off at his place and drove home to clean up. I pulled the car into the garage, shut the garage door, got out, and stripped naked. The suit, the shirt, the tie, my socks, and my drawers went into a trash bag and into the garbage can.

They should have gone to the toxic waste dump.

I was still a mess because the attempted suicide's blood was smeared on my face and arms. I went into the house, carefully. The entrance opened into the rec room on the garage level. My effort to avoid being seen was foiled by the fact that Kathy could look down from the second-floor balcony just off the kitchen.

She'd been cooking dinner and had two huge plates of food in her hands. When she saw me, she dropped it all on the floor.

"It's not my blood!" I yelled. "It's not! We had a guy try to blow his face off today."

Kathy looked down at me in horror. I'm not sure if it was still the blood, or the fact that she'd just destroyed two hours of cooking. I thought it wise not to point out that we'd probably lost our appetites anyway.

I'd lost sight of Kathy upstairs, so I waited for her to say something to make sure she hadn't fainted, or fled our marriage forever. This wasn't the first time I'd come home and scared the hell out of her.

Her voice finally came over the balcony railing, dripping with resignation and sarcasm as usual.

"It is always interesting being married to you," she said.

Sometimes it was scary, and dangerous, too.

NO ESCAPE

There must be other jobs and careers that leak into every aspect of your personal and family life, weighing on you and those you love. I'm sure many doctors and pastors are always on call and their families pay a price, too. The difference is the darkness and the violence that comes with police work. It seems to follow you everywhere you go.

As much as I tried to wall off my life at work from my life at home, there really was no way to keep them separate much of the time. It wasn't like I had a nine-to-five job where I could just leave the office, shut the door on work, then go home and shift into husband and father mode.

After I became a homicide detective and then commander of the homicide division, it was especially bad for my family. There was no closing the door after that. The home front provided little relief from the battlefront of my work, and too often my work intruded on my time with Kathy and the kids.

My wife resented it. She called my police pager "the leash" because I was always being yanked away from our family. I could see the disappointment in her eyes whenever this happened, or when she'd say, "Let's take the kids skiing this weekend" and I'd say, "I'm on call and we have this big case . . ."

She'd pack up the kids and take off, reminding me, "You work there. We don't."

The intrusions were bad enough; the outright threats were something altogether worse. I'd been a patrolman about five minutes when the first threat came to my family. It didn't bode well for the future that a death threat resulted from a mere traffic stop, though we didn't know that at first. The guy had tracked down my home number and my address and, apparently, he'd been watching the house.

I made a rookie mistake. I hadn't paid the extra monthly fee for an unlisted phone number at that point because it didn't seem plausible that someone would come after my family. This guy did.

I had just moved out of training into my own patrol car when this happened and I had no idea how quickly I'd make enemies out there. Kathy was home one night with our son and daughter, who were both toddlers, when the first anonymous call came.

"I know where you live. And you have blue carpet in the family room. I'm going to kill you and your kids."

Kathy freaked out. I couldn't blame her, especially after he called back two more times within a short time frame. She didn't call me at work at first, because she didn't want to seem like the panicky wife of a rookie cop, but when a guy threatens to kill the whole family, and calls three times, it is probably time to sound the alarm.

She called police dispatch and told them about the threats. The dispatcher told her to secure the house and that they'd have me come home right away. Kathy had a gun and she was good with it. She made sure the kids were in their cribs and that all the doors were locked. She went to our room and kept watch from the window, staying behind a curtain with the lights out.

It was late. Kathy was dressed for bed in a skimpy nightgown, bless her. She hadn't thought to get dressed, because dispatch said they were sending me home right away. While she was waiting, and watching, nervous as hell, she heard somebody rattling the window of our kid's bedroom, which was on the street level of the house.

You've heard of the Mama Bear syndrome, in which the maternal instincts kick in like an amphetamine? Kathy went into grizzly mode. She grabbed her gun and went out the front door ready to blast the bastard who'd been terrorizing her.

She saw a guy in the shadows near the kid's bedroom window, took aim, and gave him a warning, just as I'd taught her. Thank God, she remembered that part.

"I see you and you'd better come out of those bushes or I'll blow your ass away!" she said.

The guy came crashing out of the bushes with his arms in the air and it was lucky for him that my wife didn't have a jumpy trigger finger. Lucky for all of us, because he was a cop!

She still had him frozen in her sights when I came flying around the corner in my patrol car. I was going so fast when my car hit the driveway that it ripped the oil pan off. I put my lights on him.

The first thing I noticed was that he was in uniform. The second thing I noticed was that he'd pissed himself.

Yeah, Kathy could do that to a guy.

"What the hell? Kathy, put the gun down!"

"I damned near shot him," she said. "Why were you banging on the kids' bedroom window?"

The other patrolman was still shaken up. He'd been nearby when he heard dispatch send me home, so he'd been checking to make sure no one had gotten in the house.

"Kathy, give me your gun," I said.

Then I noticed for the first time that she was in her flimsy negligee.

"Geez, you're almost naked. Get in the house, please."

Kathy looked down. She'd forgotten what she had on.

"Oh shit," she said.

She handed me her Glock and scampered into the house, flashing her butt.

I went inside and got a clean pair of pants for my fellow patrol officer, who should have alerted Kathy that he was out there. I couldn't get mad at him for trying to help.

Word had spread about our caller and the other patrol cops figured out that it was some asshole I'd pulled over for speeding. They told him to clear out of town before they beat him to death. He packed his bags and never returned, as far as I knew.

There was some long-term impact on my private life from that early scare. Kathy threw out all of her sexy nighties and stocked up on flannel pajamas. That hurt more than you want to know.

I did make sure to ante up for an unlisted telephone number the next day. Even so, there would be other threats to my family and my marriage over the years. Kathy always carried her gun in her purse after that first incident. She was shopping one time when the kids were still little. They were standing in a checkout line with a shopping cart full of stuff. Kathy was unloading her cart when she noticed the woman behind her staring at her purse, which was open in the cart basket. Her gun was in clear view.

The woman looked at the kids, then the gun, then back at the kids.

"You can go ahead of me," said Kathy to the woman.

She didn't argue, and she wasted no time in checking out and leaving the store.

THE TALK OF THE NEIGHBORHOOD

We had to laugh at some of the crazy ways my job impacted our private lives. Otherwise, we'd probably have gone nuts, or filed for divorce. Even innocent things bit us on the ass. Like watching *Monday Night Football*.

Our first house in Colorado Springs was in a working-class neighborhood. We only had a one-car garage, so we kept the family vehicle in it. I had another car I drove to work, a 1958 Pontiac Safari station wagon that I bought for twenty-five dollars. It was such a junker, our vice squad would borrow it when they went trolling for street hookers on weekends. They took to calling it "the Hooker Huntin' Wagon," which Kathy didn't find amusing, at all.

Anyway, my work car wasn't marked as a police car. We hadn't gotten to know our neighbors yet, so none of them knew I was a cop. So they didn't know what to think when our driveway filled up with police squad cars on Monday nights.

This was back when *Monday Night Football* on television was new and a big deal, with Howard Cosell, Frank Gifford, and Don Meredith calling the games. The six patrolmen who worked in our side of town would grab some fast-food burgers and fries and head to our house for their Monday night dinner breaks, so they could catch a little of the game each week. It got to be a regular thing.

Apparently, the neighbors noticed. One day this older lady from down the street, whom Kathy had never met, stopped her while she was walking with the kids in a stroller.

"Hello, my dear," said the lady, putting her hand on my wife's arm.

This was the friendliest she'd ever been, so Kathy knew something was up.

The woman paused a second, gave Kathy a very serious and concerned look, and said, "Honey, if you and your husband have any more problems on Monday nights, you can feel free to bring the kids to our house before the police get there."

Kathy broke out in laughter, which mortified the lady.

"I'm sorry," my wife said. "I know you were trying to be helpful, but you see all those police cars at our house because my husband is a cop and his friends on the force come over to watch a little of *Monday Night Football* every week."

The woman felt awful, but she was comforted to learn I wasn't beating the crap out of my wife at halftime.

HOME INVASION

By the time I became a detective and, later, a supervisor over several divisions, the neighbors and most other people in town saw my face on television and in the newspaper on a regular basis. It was no secret what I did for a living. People recognized me everywhere I went and it became a problem.

I rarely went out in public with my family, but when I did go there was usually some sort of encounter. Kathy and Kris and I were in the mall on one rare visit and this woman came rushing up while bawling uncontrollably. Her husband was standing behind her with a mortified look on his face, shifting from one foot to the next.

"You were so good to me when my daughter was murdered," the woman said while hugging me.

I gently broke her grip and said something inane, I'm sure, before patting her on the shoulder and walking away.

Kathy said, "Who was that? When was her daughter murdered?"

"I'm embarrassed to tell you that I have no idea," I said. I saw a lot of murdered daughters.

You can be an accountant or a car salesman from nine to five, but a cop is always a cop. I guess we are like priests in that way, if not in any others. We'd go to parties and you could hear the host couple and guests flushing their pot and other illicit drugs down the toilet as we walked in the front door. That was always amusing.

Not so amusing were the invasions of our privacy by the media and others. On several occasions the hounds of the local media would get overexcited at the scent of a big story, a multiple homicide or sensational sex case. If they couldn't find me at work, where I was adept at hiding from them, they would sometimes dare to show up on my doorstep or in my yard at home.

This did not go over well.

I was having dinner with Kathy and the kids, who were then teenagers. The doorbell rang. I went to the front door, opened it, and was blinded by television camera lights. They lit up our front entry hall like it was the White House press briefing room.

I was so furious, I couldn't speak at first.

I know you find that hard to believe, but it is God's honest truth.

My son later told Kathy that he'd never before seen me yell at someone without moving my lips. He always was very perceptive.

I didn't move my lips because I was gritting my teeth while I told those sons of bitches to get the hell off my porch and out of my yard. It was a reporter and cameraman from the only station in town that had the balls to send someone to my home. They'd apparently dispatched the youngest and newest reporter, who was deaf as well as dumb.

He stood his ground while his camera guide aimed his lens, his light, and his microphone in my face. I glared at him with my best death-ray stare and through clenched lips asked a question.

"Do you have a string tied to that camera?" I asked.

"Why?" said the rookie reporter.

"Because after I stick the camera up your ass, it will be easier for you to pull it out with the string," I said. "Now get the fuck off my porch or I will kill you and all of your relatives. And if you put this video on television, I will make it a point to go after all of your descendants for the next three generations."

I was once known for my bad temper. They were lucky I'd been working on mellowing it out. But I wasn't done with this reporting team, yet.

After they drove off, I grabbed the house phone and I called the news director who'd dispatched him to my door. I knew how these things worked. That kid hadn't come on his own.

My message to him was this: "It is of absolutely no interest to me if anyone in this world watches your nightly news, but if you ever send your pack of morons to my private home again, your station will be banned from the police station and any of our news conferences."

I didn't give him the opportunity to respond, because I had more to say: "You probably have never given thought to the fact that there are hundreds of criminals out there who would love to know where I live so they could do harm to my family and me, but I think about it every day because they constantly threaten to do just that. If bad things happen to us, bad things, much worse things, will happen to you.

"As of right now, you and your station are on probation. I will not speak to any of your employees for thirty days. Your reporters and cameramen will be ignored at crime scenes. No questions will be entertained. No statements shared. We'll see how you like that."

The station manager called my chief of police to complain and the chief, bless him, hung up on him. All of the other stations piled on and openly criticized the one who'd sent a crew to my house. They were sucking up, but that worked for me.

DETECTIVE DAD

The kids were impacted in many ways by my job and the stress of my daily encounters with death, deviance, and all of the darkest aspects of humanity. Dan and Kris will tell you that while I lashed out at them in anger, my mood was perpetually sour due to stress, overwork, and overexposure to evil. Their friends all knew what I did for a living because they'd see me on television or in the newspapers. They also knew to keep the racket down when they came to the house because I was either sleeping or desperately in need of sleep. They were very quiet and respectful around me, which Dan credits to my "grim intensity."

Kris remembers that my dating advice was "a bit unconventional." She recalls this tidbit from her doting father as she entered high school:

> "Whenever you think you might be getting serious about someone you are dating, ask them about the crazy members of their family. Every family has them. They should be comfortable sharing their concerns, but if they tell you they don't have any crazy family members, then guess what? You are talking to the crazy one!"

My wife and kids did reap a few perks from having a cop in the family. Kathy is the daughter of a car dealer. Her dad owned several dealerships as she was growing up, so once she earned her driver's license she always had nice cars. She also drove them like she was racking up NASCAR points.

She had her dainty lead foot on the gas pedal at all times, and she didn't feel bound by the rules of the road. She was pulled over once for making an illegal turn. I was a patrol sergeant at the time. While the officer was filling out her ticket, he looked at her driver's license. His pen froze in midair.

"Ma'am, are you related to Sergeant Joe Kenda?"

"Yes, he's my husband. Why?"

He snapped shut his writing pad and handed back her license.

"Lady, I wouldn't write you a ticket on a *bet*!"

Case closed.

Another one of our traffic officers wasn't so lenient, especially after he'd seen Kathy exceeding the speed limit around town several times. He knew me, but he didn't know her.

Officer Kenny Jones was a motorcycle cop and a good one. One day he pulled Kathy over for exceeding the speed limit. She handed him her license. He examined it and said, "Should I know this last name?"

Kathy smiled slyly and said, "You might."

Kenny removed his sunglasses and looked at our kids in the backseat of Kathy's car. He then reached into his uniform shirt pocket, pulled out his police department business card, and handed it to my son.

"Here you go, kids, this has my work phone number on it," he said. "Whenever your mommy speeds again, call me and I will come buy you each an ice cream cone."

Officer Jones was a wise man. From that day forward, our kids monitored the speedometer and the speed limit whenever they were in the car with Kathy. Once the needle moved beyond the limit, they began chanting, "*Ice cream! Ice cream! Ice cream!*"

Nothing slows a mother down like two shrieking kiddies in the backseat.

PARENTAL POLICING

My son, Dan, also benefited from professional courtesy among law enforcement officers, although he didn't see it that way at the time. Like our daughter, he was a good kid, actually a great kid, who played sports, hung out with his buddies, and enjoyed the company of the opposite sex. Apparently they enjoyed his company, too.

When he was fifteen, Dan had his mother drop him off at the downtown mall. He told Kathy that he planned to meet a girl and go to a movie with her. Except, Dan talked the girl into skipping the movie. Instead they went for a walk and found a little park, where they proceeded to do what teenage boys and girls do.

A mall cop found them both naked from the waist up. He also found Dan's buck knife lying next to him in the grass, which raised some suspicions. Dan had taken it out of his back pocket because it was jabbing his butt. The mall cop cuffed him.

While Dan's girlfriend put her clothes back on, the mall cop called our department. Word got around. I was notified that my bare-chested son had been apprehended with a seminude underage girl and a weapon. It sounded worse than it was, of course, but at the time I wondered if they had the right kid.

I drove to the mall and found them in the park. Dan was trying to hide behind a tree, or climb inside the tree. I could tell that he thought he'd be grounded for life and maybe chained to a post in the basement until graduation. In truth, I could hardly keep from laughing and slapping him on his bare back. However, I did maintain a paternal scowl while getting the cuffs removed, and his shirt on.

After we dropped his friend off, I managed to give him a good stern talking-to about treating young women with respect, and keeping his buck knife, among other things, in his pants. Then I returned to work and accepted congratulations from my coworkers.

Both of our kids seemed to have inherited or at least absorbed through osmosis the "serve and protect" mentality that I brought to police work and their mother brought to her own career as a nurse. As adults, Dan and Kris have high-level military jobs that involve protecting our nation. Even as teenagers, they were very responsible and protective of those around them.

THE BALLAD OF JOE AND YUKO AND KRIS

I came home late from work one night when Kris was seventeen. She was five feet four inches tall with an alligator mouth. I have no idea where she got it, but she was a very assertive young lady. You didn't mess with her unless you were suicidal.

When I walked in the front door, my wife gave me a death stare and said, "You'd better sit down."

I hated that expression.

Kris came around a corner. I could tell she was all hyped up. She let loose with her super-serious "*Daaaaaad!*"

My first thought was a father's nightmare: *She's pregnant with twins!*

Just then, around the corner came what I first thought was some sort of apparition: a four-foot, six-inch teenage Asian female who was bowing to me and crying simultaneously. Her weeping increased as Kris began explaining her presence in our home.

I'd had a tough day on the job. My mind was having a hard time handling this strange moment on the home front. My thoughts wandered. *Am I in the right house? Is this a dream? That is my daughter, but who is this sobbing Asian girl and why is she flooding our family room with tears?*

Kris laid it out as if she were typing up a report for the duty sergeant.

"Dad, this is Yuko Yamahira from Osaka, Japan. She is an exchange student at school. I met her at lunch today in the cafeteria. She was crying and I asked what was wrong."

Kris told me that Yuko had been assigned to her host family here by some placement service. She didn't know this family. They had no connection. Yuko had just realized that her host mother was forging her name and stealing the postal money orders that were being sent to her by her family back in Japan. Her host mother had stolen six hundred dollars, so far. She had also taken most of Yuko's clothing and distributed it to her own children.

Yuko cried through this entire presentation. At least now I knew what had inspired the flood of tears. Before I could promise to look into this, excuse myself, and crawl into bed, my daughter slapped a manila folder on the coffee table. I made a mental note to confiscate all of her Nancy Drew mystery novels at the next opportunity.

She'd been investigating Yuko's case all day. She had copies of the forged signatures on Yuko's postal money orders.

"How did you get these?"

Yuko had asked Kris to take her to the post office. She had a letter addressed to her from her mother in Japan. Yuko had found the letter insider her host mother's purse, opened. She knew that her real mother back home had sent the letter with cash in it for her. It was sent certified mail, requiring the recipient's signature. Yuko realized her host mother must have forged her signature and then stolen the cash. She asked Kris to take her to the post office so she could see for sure who had signed her name on the ledger.

Kris drove her to the post office, after sweet-talking her French teacher into letting her skip class. While Yuko was bowing and averting her eyes and being the polite, nonaccusatory Japanese young lady, my daughter went all *Blue Steel*, demanding to see the postmaster. The fifty-year-old bureaucrat came to the window, clearly not impressed with the teenage duo.

Yuko spoke at first, trying to explain through her tears what she wanted, without making any accusations. Between her accented English and her sobs, the postmaster couldn't understand her. He was losing patience fast.

Then Kris stepped up to the plate, swinging from the hips.

"We need to look at the signature ledger for certified mail," she said. "We suspect that her host mother signed for a letter and took money that was intended for her."

He presented the ledger. Yuko confirmed that it was not her signature. The postmaster went ballistic.

"THIS is FRAUD of the United States Postal Service! We are going to get the POLICE involved, and get to the bottom of THIS!"

Yuko freaked out.

Kris pulled the Dad card.

"Sir, my father *is* the police. Let me talk to him; I'll have him call you."

They left with a photocopy of the forged signature in Kris's little case folder. They came home and waited for unsuspecting me. After hearing their story, I promised to look into it in the morning. Yuko spent the night with us, with my blessing.

The next day, I first went to the post office to see what other evidence I could gather of the mother's crimes. I explained that I was following up on a complaint and that he'd talked to a Japanese girl and her friend the day before.

"Oh yeah," said the postmaster, "that little white girl took over the place. When they told her that I was too busy to talk to her, she said, 'I didn't ask you if he was busy, I told you I wanted to see him, now!' Who was that kid?"

I explained that she was a chip off my own block.

The postmaster and I had a talk with his idiot postal employee who allowed Yuko's clearly non-Japanese host mother to sign for her certified mail. I got his statement and his identification of the woman.

I then drove to the host mother's house and recovered Yuko's clothing as well as most of the cash she'd taken. It was midnight before I returned home.

Yuko was still there, still weeping, while standing next to a suitcase the size of a Buick station wagon. Another strange person was also present. He turned out to be the placement officer for the foreign exchange program. He said that because of what had taken place, he was prepared to place Yuko with another family.

Yuko bowed to me, wiping tears from her face.

My daughter gave me "the look." Kathy backed her up.

"Okay, she can have Dan's room since he's gone off to college," I said.

She lived with us for the rest of the school year and proved to be a great kid. She is now an accountant with KPMG in Osaka. She still calls us "Mom and Dad."

Her exceedingly grateful parents, who owned an insurance company and were quite wealthy, kept sending us outrageously expensive gifts on a weekly basis, until I asked them to please stop.

THE SHIT MAGNET: FAMILY VACATION VERSION

You've no doubt heard the psychologists' adage that if the only tool you have is a hammer, everything looks like a nail. Well, I sometimes wondered if it worked the same way for cops: *Once you put on a badge, everyone begins to look like a criminal.*

Too often, people I ran into during my off-hours actually were criminals. The foreign exchange student's host mom was only one example of this. I mean, how many people bring foreign teenagers halfway across the world so they can rob them?

Then there was a rare night out with Kathy and her fellow nurse friend. My wife wasn't happy that we rarely went out for a fun evening, because I was either working or exhausted from working. One night I came home and she was giving me the dreaded narrow blue-eyed squint. I knew I was in trouble. Then she used my last name. Confirmed.

"Kenda! We never go anywhere because all you do is hang out with dead people all day, you son of a bitch! I want to go hang out with some people who are alive and breathing. So, we are going dancing. You and me!"

So we went to this sprawling country bar back when *Urban Cowboy* was big and all these joints had electronic bulls and certified public accountants wearing tight jeans, boots, and Stetsons. Kathy wanted to learn how to do the two-step dance. I went along for the two-drinks-for-the-price-of-one dance.

We were joined by a nurse friend of hers from work and the woman's husband. Kathy didn't know the woman or the husband very well. I didn't know them at all. When we met up, my impression was that she was about twenty years older than him. She looked about forty, him about half that.

Well, cradle robbing was not a crime, so I just smiled and said hello.

We walked into the bar and the temperature dropped about 20 degrees because my face has been on the news so many times that everyone assumed I was there to bust up the party. A lot of people suddenly ran to the restrooms.

I was off duty, so all I cared about was my own refreshments.

We'd been there a short time when the young husband wandered off. His wife waited for him to get clear, then she grabbed my arm and bent my ear.

"Joe, I need to talk to you about my daughter," she said.

Oh, here we go, I thought.

The daughter was seventeen, hers from a previous marriage, not his. She'd always been a good student and good kid, until two years ago, when her attitude took a turn for the worse—even more than most teenagers. She started doing drugs, skipping school, and spending nights away from home.

"What changed in your household two years ago?" I asked.

I was hoping her answer wouldn't be what I'd suspected.

"Well, that's when I met my him, my new husband," she said.

That was the answer I'd hoped not to hear.

Just then, he came back to the table.

Kathy was ready to go try the Texas two-step, but I'd shifted into work mode, thanks to her pal's concerns about the daughter.

The husband was right there, so I asked him: "Your wife says she's been having trouble with her daughter since you two hooked up."

He pretended not to hear me and instead took a swig of his drink.

You son of a bitch, I thought.

Kathy was pushing me to dance. I squeezed her thigh so hard, she nearly yelped out loud.

I said to our tablemates, "Kathy and I have to go home."

Then I handed her nurse friend my business card.

"You need to come to my office in the morning with your daughter. Just the two of you. Don't be late or I will come and find you."

She turned white.

The husband didn't acknowledge our departure. If he'd been smart, he would have left town that night. He wasn't that smart.

The mother and daughter came in the next morning. I had invited a youth counselor experienced in dealing with teens who've been sexually assaulted and abused. The counselor was very talented and knew how to get victims to talk to her about horrible experiences. They spoke for an hour and a half.

The new husband had been sexually abusing her ever since he moved in. She had bruises and other physical evidence. The mother claimed she had had no idea. I had no proof otherwise, but her daughter was removed from her custody. I arrested the husband on multiple charges of sexual assault and abuse of a minor.

That night I went home and told Kathy that I'd arrested her friend's husband and arranged for her daughter to be put in foster care.

"So, you want to go learn to tango next week?" I asked.

My wife threw a coffee cup at me. She missed.

I didn't arrest all of Kathy's friends, just some of them, or their family members every now and then. Our work lives did seem to cross over frequently.

While on duty at the hospital, Kathy had to wear the required ID with her name on it. There weren't any other Kendas in Colorado Springs, so when people saw her badge, they made the connection. Every now and then she'd have to tell her supervisors that she couldn't care for a patient because I'd put him in the hospital in the first place.

She was "Franny Float" because she could handle anything. She floated from one department to the next depending on where they needed her. She might be in ICU one day, the pediatric wing on another, and then the emergency room the next.

One day, a big orderly named Michael got in Kathy's face. She'd known him a long time, and they'd always gotten along, but she'd never seen him like this.

"Your husband killed my brother last night," he said, glaring at her.

Kathy was pretty quick on her feet, and she was not easily intimidated.

"I don't know what happened between your brother and my husband, but you and I have never had a problem," she said. "Does this mean there will be a problem?"

"No," he said, walking away.

That night, she asked for an explanation. It took me a minute to make the connection. I hadn't killed anyone that I knew of, but it had been a busy few days.

Then I figured it out. The brother's name was Gilbert. I'd tracked him down fifty-two hours after he'd murdered five people in an armed robbery and set a business on fire. We learned that he was hiding out in an apartment. We surrounded it.

I called him and told him to surrender.

He put the phone down and I heard him say something to a woman in the background. She screamed, "The police!" Apparently Gilbert had not told her of his crime spree.

The next thing I heard was him breathing heavily a couple of times, and then a loud bang. SWAT went in. I was afraid he'd shot the woman, but she was standing with her hands in the air, covered in Gilbert's blood.

She was wearing panties and screaming like a banshee. He'd shot himself with a .357 and blown off his skullcap. I told Kathy to tell his brother that I didn't pull the trigger, but I was talking to him on the phone when he turned out his own lights.

Once again, she wasn't amused.

Occasions like that may have been the reason my wife once had me thrown out of her hospital, blowing my cover for the rest of my career. I'd taught myself how to read medical charts and, as I mentioned earlier, I'd also become fairly adept at pretending to be a doctor. One day, I was on her hospital's seventh-floor surgical recovery room, snooping around and reading the chart of a guy who was a suspect in a murder case.

Who should walk by, but my beloved spouse?

"What the hell are you doing?" she asked.

I detected no matrimonial warmth in her question.

"What's it look like I'm doing?" I said.

"It looks like you are breaking the law by reading a private medical record, you asshole," she said.

A supervisory nurse walked by and caught the last part of Kathy's comment.

"You shouldn't talk to a doctor that way," the supervisor said.

"He's not a doctor, he's a cop," said Kathy.

"How do you know?" asked the supervisor.

"Because he's my husband."

I gave my wife the death stare.

Her supervisor threatened to call security.

By then I knew what was on the chart, so I retired from practicing medicine and went back to the cop shop. It made for an interesting conversation at dinner that night.

SHIT MAGNET FAMILY VACATION

My reputation for attracting trouble had become well established at work and at home by 1990. My fellow officers knew it, and my family knew it. One way or another, they'd all been witness to the fact that I was a bona fide shit magnet.

Even so, you'd think that I'd be able to take a break from crime on a family vacation. Wouldn't you?

I was still six years from retirement when Kathy, Kris, and I drove 1,200 miles to visit son Dan in San Diego while he was doing his ROTC summer training on a naval base there. We'd never been to Southern California so this seemed like a great opportunity to get out of the Rockies and head to the West Coast.

We booked a room at a Holiday Inn near the San Diego harbor and Navy Pier. After we checked in, we had a few hours before we could meet up with Dan, so Kathy, Kris, and I went for a walk along the waterfront. We were looking at all the yachts, sailboats, and commercial vessels docked in the harbor, and enjoying a much different view than we had back home, when Kathy pointed to an unusual boat that had a big for-sale sign on it.

The large commercial boat was all lit up so it stood out in the darkness. It also had what looked like construction boom cranes looming at the rear, with large nets draped from them.

As we walked by it, Kathy said, "I wonder what kind of boat it is?"

"It's a tuna seiner," said a voice. "You can buy it today for eight million dollars."

We hadn't seen a little old guy sitting in a folding chair on the dock near the boat's gangway. He was a friendly guy of Portuguese descent, in his seventies, who said he'd been a member of the crew for years and was now serving as the night watchman while it was docked and on the market.

He asked where we were from and when we told him, he said his daughter lived in Castle Rock, between Denver and Colorado Springs. We chatted for forty-five minutes or so. He was an interesting guy. As we were preparing to move on, I took out a business card and slid it into his shirt pocket.

"When you come to visit your daughter, give us a call and we'll go out to dinner," I said.

Just then, a ratty-looking piece of crap, a blueish Chevy Impala, probably about twenty-five years old, rolled by slowly. Its headlights were not on, which struck me as strange. My bad-guy radar went off when I saw the two shady characters in the front seat, a pair of young Hispanic males, who were glaring at us. The night watchman stood up when he saw them coming.

I saw fear in his eyes as he stepped behind me. There was something going on between him and these two guys, and it seemed bad enough that I found myself wishing I'd brought my gun. After they rolled on by, I watched the car do a U-turn. They came by again, a little faster, but not much.

The old guy stayed behind me. After they'd gone out of sight, I asked him, "What was that about?"

He explained that the two guys in the car had been on the boat's crew, too. They'd lost their jobs because the boat was being sold, but they wanted to sleep on board. The night watchman had refused to let them do that. Now they were harassing him on a regular basis.

"If you see them coming back again, call 911," I told him. "Let the local cops know that they are threatening you. I get the feeling they aren't fooling around."

We then said our goodbyes and we walked back to the hotel. I was nagged by concerns all night. The next morning, we went for a harbor cruise on a tourist sightseeing boat. When we reached the marina, we saw yellow police tape around the tuna seiner. There were squad cars and some unmarked police cars nearby.

"I'll bet those dirtbags came back and shot the night watchman," I told Kathy.

My first thought was sadness for the nice old guy. My second thought was that the San Diego cops were probably looking for me. I had no doubt they'd found my business card in his shirt pocket and wondered what the connection might be.

We walked back to my hotel room and I called my office. They said San Diego detectives had already been trying to locate me. My next call was to the San Diego Police Department. The operator transferred me to their homicide division.

"Detective Kenda, we've been looking for you," said their supervisor. "We found your card on our victim last night."

He confirmed that the night watchman had been killed.

"I'll be glad to talk to your guys and tell them what I know," I said.

They sent two detectives to our hotel. They probably weren't hoping for much, so they were a little surprised when I gave them a thorough description of the two guys and their junky car.

"Do you want the license number on the plate?" I asked.

Veteran detectives keep their emotions in check, but I could tell they were peeing themselves as I gave them the tag number. Anytime my radar goes off on a car, I memorize the plate and keep it in a file somewhere in my dark and twisted mind.

They were very grateful. Two weeks later they called and said they had caught the two former crew members and charged them with the murder of the night watchman. I thought we might have to go back to testify in court, but the killers pleaded guilty and went to prison without any more of my help.

Kathy and the kids must have rolled their eyes for a week after I solved a murder on vacation. The guys back at work said this only confirmed that my shit magnet never rested.

RETIREMENT WAS MURDER UNTIL MY SECOND LIFE OF CRIME

We were having an exceptionally bad day in the major crimes division. The phones were ringing off the wall. Everybody was yelling at each other. Irate mothers, pissed-off fathers, angry victims, crazed addicts; the lobby was filled with raging lunatics. And I'd run out of detectives.

I was the lieutenant in charge and one of my units was sex crimes. We had arrested a seventy-year-old man for sexually assaulting his five-year-old grandson. I had nobody to interview him. So I took him.

I joined the suspect in the interview room and I went straight to the point.

"What made you touch that little boy?"

"He came on to me."

The next thing I remember was someone tugging hard on my shoulders and arms and a voice saying, "Lieutenant! Lieutenant!"

They'd pulled me off the grandfather on the floor. I was strangling him. He'd turned blue and just about checked out when they pried my hands from his neck.

"Get him to Medical and out of my sight," I said.

My gut was churning. I went back to my office and took a minute. Then I typed a one-page, one-line, interoffice memorandum to the chief of police. *Please accept my retirement request.* This was in the winter of 1996.

When I signed it, I felt like someone had lifted an aircraft carrier off my shoulders.

I didn't walk out of there, I floated. I was lighter than air. I was euphoric, absolutely euphoric.

I went home, walked in the door, and told Kathy: "I'm done. I retired."

It was not that guy on that particular day. It was every guy. It was every day. It was all the pain and suffering, and hearing all the lies and all the terrible excuses and all the ridiculous claims of innocence I'd been told over the years.

He came on to me.

A grandfather claiming that he'd molested his grandson because the kid asked for it?

I lost it in the moment, but I'd been losing it for quite a while. Kathy was done with it and now I was, too.

I could no longer separate my emotions from my work. I'd feared this moment would come. For the first time in twenty-three and a half years on the job, my emotions had overwhelmed my judgment. I'd sworn that would never happen to me. It was time to walk, time to get out of police work before I did something really stupid.

There was no retirement ceremony for me, because I didn't want one. I was there one day and not the next. Time for a new chapter. I couldn't tell another parent that a child wasn't coming home. I couldn't talk to another grieving mother. I couldn't look at another dead person lying in blood. I had reached my emotional limit. Everything around me had become white noise. I had tuned out the world around me, along with my own humanity.

KATHY'S TURN

Kathy had been pushing me to retire for a long time before that. She'd become convinced that I would be killed on the job. She'd seen too many news reports with lines like this: "He was only two weeks from retirement when he was shot in the face during a routine traffic stop."

She was sick to death of waiting for that telephone call. She knew my odds were running out. She was afraid I'd get killed, do something stupid and get shot, and not be with her in retirement.

When I made the rank of lieutenant, I could have sent my minions out to arrest people while I went to meetings and stayed at my desk, but I didn't do that. I had signed up to kick in doors and put bad people away and that is what I liked to do. I liked being on the street with my officers and detectives. I didn't want to ask them to do what I wasn't willing to do. That annoyed Kathy no end as time went on.

She thought I was being unfair to her, and she was right. The worst part of that is I knew it and I didn't care. I didn't care who else it was good or bad for until that last moment when I did care about her and me and our future together. There were days and nights on the job when I seriously thought I was on the precipice of death.

I'd be under fire. People were trying to kill me. I had no tactical advantage. I couldn't see the guy shooting at me and all I could do was hope he stopped pumping rounds. I would think about my mortality in those moments.

Do you want to leave Kathy a widow with a police pension and your name on a memorial wall?

I didn't want her to face that. She had been to police funerals with me. I buried seven friends killed on the job, or by the job. I always saw this stricken look on Kathy's face at those funerals. I knew what she was thinking: *I hope I'm never at one of these alone.*

One night I came home after working a case five days straight. There'd been a shooting with a machine gun. I told her I was going after the suspect early one night and then I didn't get back until 1 a.m. The lights were on in the house and that wasn't normal for the hour.

Kathy was never up that late. I found her in the living room with a drink in front of her, which also was rare. She was crying. I thought maybe her mother had died, but she was crying because she was really pissed at me.

"Kenda, I can't wait for you to come home anymore," she said. "I can't live twenty-four hours a day thinking about you getting killed anymore. I'd always had to shut out that thought and continue with life. The kids go to school. I'd go to work, come home, and fix the plumbing because you weren't around. It's wasn't on my mind twenty-four hours a day, but sometimes when the kids were in bed and I was alone at night having a glass of wine, the thought would overwhelm me and I'd find myself saying it aloud: "I hope he's okay. I hope tonight isn't the night."

I hadn't spent much one-on-one time with Kathy over all the years of raising the kids and both of us working. We put in long hours. She was looking forward to having time together. It was her turn. I was selfish to stay on so long. I was bringing the emotional burden of my work home.

I made sure I never left the house without saying "I love you" because it might have been the last time I saw her. I still do that today, but it had a different meaning then. For too long, the pain I brought into my family didn't matter as much as my addiction to the adrenaline high of chasing killers. Like any addiction, though, there was a price to pay. Everything else in my life became secondary. I didn't hear their pleas to quit. It was all white noise. I shut down emotionally.

Here's Kathy:

I had to keep the kids quiet during the day, and when he was on swing shift the kids weren't there. Police, firemen, nurses, a lot of people work those hours, so that wasn't abnormal, but when he got into homicide it changed. I could never be sure he would be home. He usually worked the day shift, but anytime there was a homicide they called and he was gone.

So, I always had a babysitter for the kids whether he was in home or in bed. I never relied on him to be there, because we never knew when he'd get called out. He'd call and say I just got a homicide. I won't be home for dinner and I'd see him when I'd see him. He worked. I worked. There were times when we communicated mostly through messages stuck to the refrigerator with magnets.

I learned to sleep soundly; only the kids woke me up. If I waited for him, I'd never get sleep. Sometimes I'd be walking out with the kids, taking them to the babysitter and he'd be walking in from a long night, hoping to sleep for a while.

Fortunately, I pulled out before I became like the animals I'd hunted. Then something I hadn't anticipated happened. Retirement nearly killed me. The day after I retired, I woke up and it was like, *What have I done?*

The reality of it takes a while to settle in. I was disoriented. I didn't know what to do with myself for the first few days. You live with heavy family, financial, and work responsibilities for a long time, the things that keep you motivated to stay on the job, and then when they are gone, you have to adjust.

I'd think about what I had to do and then I'd realize, *Hey, our kids are out of college now. I quit the department. They will all survive without me. All I have to do is keep us alive.*

We had saved money for twenty years by never living beyond our means. We paid for our kids' educations—I don't know how we did that, really. We didn't have a lot of debt and I had a decent pension. I knew we were okay financially if we remained conservative. I just didn't know if I could take it emotionally.

Murder victims haunted me: The cases I didn't solve. The cases I did solve. They reached out from the grave for me. I'd built a shield made of railroad steel around my heart, but my memories were like armor-piercing bullets. They were triggered again and again—by a smell, a sound, a face from the past—and then the shield was shattered.

Kathy and I were watching a nice television report on a former policewoman who taught kids how to read on her time off. It was a heartwarming, upbeat story.

I bolted from my easy chair, looked at Kathy, and said, "I have to go outside." She had learned to leave me alone in those moments.

Twenty years earlier, I'd had a murder case involving a little boy. Horrible things had been done to him. One of the kids in the television report looked just like that boy. I knew it wasn't him, but when I saw his face, the memories shot right through my heart. I was back at the murder scene in seconds.

Those memories and feelings still pop up. It's the price I pay for the work I did at a high level of intensity for so many years. After I retired, Kathy and I would designate certain nights to sit at the kitchen table. She'd let me talk late into the night. That helped some. I'd feel better for a while.

POLICE TRAUMATIC STRESS DISORDER

The best description of post-traumatic stress disorder I can give you is that it's like having a nightmare while you are awake. My dead people began to visit me day and night. I wasn't doing well in my first few months of retirement. I'd been too busy and too tired and too numbed when I was still on the job. The memories were walled off. Then they weren't.

Kathy, who'd also worked as a psychiatric nurse, diagnosed me with PTSD after repeated episodes of flashbacks by day and nightmares by night. My wife's professional evaluation was summed up succinctly: "You have PTSD big-time."

I didn't argue with her. I needed help.

She found a top-notch psychiatrist, not a psychologist, but a real M.D. in Denver who was supposed to be "the dude" for PTSD treatment. My health coverage wouldn't pay for mental health issues. It was four hundred dollars an hour to see him and that was a big bite out of my retirement check. I wasn't a rock star, I was a public employee.

I went anyway. I didn't want to keep driving Kathy nuts, and it wasn't much fun for me, either. This shit felt way too real and it was fogging my brain.

I went to see the shrink after paying in advance for the first session. He seemed like a nice guy. First off, he asked me if I was having recurring dreams.

"Five of them," I replied.

"Tell me about them," he said.

For the next twenty-minutes of my four-hundred-dollar hour, I told him about these nightmares and daymares that were haunting me. By the time, I was done, he was crying.

Not me, the patient. Him, the doctor.

I spent the next ten minutes comforting my psychiatrist because he was so distressed by my dreams.

All the while, I'm thinking, *What's wrong with this picture?*

I'm also thinking, *To whom do I speak about getting back my four hundred goddamn dollars?*

When I returned home, Kathy asked how it went.

"Don't ever ask me to do *that* again," I said.

MY FIVE NIGHTMARES

Let's see if my nightmares make *you* cry. The first is really sick, so brace yourself, or go read *People* magazine instead. (How are the Kardashians doing, by the way? Has Kim recovered from the burglary in Paris?)

Nightmare No. 1: I'm on the banks of a river and dead people are floating by. It's a river of death and the dead floating in it are waving at me and saying "Hi Joe!" as they float past in various stages of decomposition. The river is packed with their bodies.

In the dream, I go to turn around and leave the riverbank, but there is a wall that is one thousand feet high. I can't leave. I have to stay. There is no escape. So I stay, watching the dead float by until I finally wake up or snap out of it.

Nightmare No. 2: I walk into an apartment and find a woman dead with multiple gunshot wounds. Two in the face and three in the chest. She is not decomposed, she is a fresh kill. Part of her face is missing.

I'm there with detectives and she sits up in the bed, looks at me, and says, "You are Detective Kenda, aren't you? You have to find the person who did this to me." Everyone else leaves the room screaming. I try, but my legs won't move. She stops talking and lies down. Everyone comes back in.

"She stopped talking to me," I explain.

"What are you talking about?" the other detectives ask.

Yes, I know what you, the reader, are thinking, and you are right: I am nuts.

Nightmare No. 3: This involves the boy who was murdered by his suicidal father. The child was wearing Mickey Mouse pajamas when I found him. My own son had the same pajamas and they weren't far apart in age, so that case really got to me at the time. Apparently, it stayed with me.

In this nightmare, I find myself in a conference room. It is painted white. Everything in the room is white: the chairs, the table, the walls, the ceiling. It is so bright you can't tell where the walls and floors meet. There is a giant conference table and around it are sitting thirty or so of the victims from my cases. They are in various stages of decomposition, with clothes tattered and insects crawling on them. They all speak to me and ask me questions.

Why didn't you find who did this to me? How did you let my killer get away?

The last victim to speak is the five-year-old in Mickey pajamas. He looks at me with his remaining eye and says, "Why did you let my daddy hurt me?"

I usually wake up then. I have to walk around awhile to shake it off. It is the torture that comes with my line of work.

Nightmare No. 4: I'm looking into a refrigerator and the crisper drawer slides open on its own to reveal the head of the woman whose husband murdered and beheaded her during a psychotic episode. Her open, glazed eyes stare up at me, forcing me to relive one of the more horrifying sights of my career.

Nightmare No. 5: I'm in the morgue, looking at the wall of body drawers, and I hear a faint knocking. It doesn't come from one specific drawer; the knocking is coming from inside each and every one of them.

I hear muffled voices from inside all of the body drawers. They are calling for help. Terrified, I look around the morgue and there are bodies everywhere, jumping from one examining table to the next.

Then I wake up.

Wouldn't you?

The nightmares are always the same, though the scenarios may vary slightly. I have a few others that are less regular, but no less disturbing. One is a flashback to a girl whose body we found in the

Garden of the Gods public park. It was summer, hot and sticky. She'd been dead three weeks. We had just found her body and as we were examining it, a large beetle came out of her ear canal.

In the nightmare, the beetle stands on its hind legs, puts its little arms on its little hips, and says, "We found her and we are keeping her!"

Yeah, a talking beetle. Go ahead and say it. Kenda is bug-fuckin' crazy.

No screenwriter could come up with the scary stuff of my dreams, because they are rooted in reality. No movie or television show can put horrors in your head like that. I see it all in my dreams, every detail, and I smell it, too. A freshly killed body smells of blood, like copper, and if the deceased had been drinking, you can smell the alcohol, too, not to mention the putrid smell of decomposition. My dreams attack all of my senses as well as my mind.

My dreams have not diminished over the years. They won't.

Two months after my experience with the overly empathetic psychiatrist, I was playing golf with my former Colorado Springs police chief, who'd once been a homicide detective in Los Angeles. He's seen as much as I'd seen, maybe more.

I respected him, even though he has always insisted on calling me "Joey the K."

While we were riding in our golf cart, he asked, "Joey the K, how are you sleeping, now that you are retired?"

"I don't sleep," I said.

"You know, Joey, all that shit, it never goes away."

That moment provided an epiphany for me.

Another veteran cop with his own nightmares was telling me, "Don't fight it. Figure out how to live with it."

And I have. Just as many, many other men and women who've lived through similar horrors, or worse, have learned to do. When I talk to military veterans who've been in combat, they say the same thing: You have to learn to deal with it. You won't forget. You just learn to carry on with life.

The only difference between their horrific war experiences and mine on the street is that I had twenty-three and a half years of exposure to my nightmares. Mine was a very slow dance. For example, several years ago I was asked to testify as an expert witness and it required that I tell the court how many autopsies I'd attended as a professional witness, which was part of my job. I had the coroner's office in Colorado Springs run the numbers.

Their total was 528. That's how many autopsies I attended, officially.

A pretty high body count for one man, wouldn't you agree?

OUT OF DARKNESS AND INTO THE LIGHT

Two years after I retired, I was sitting at home in the kitchen, minding my own business, when my wife looked at me with a benevolent smile.

"Hi," she said, pleasantly.

Puzzled by this, I reminded her that I'd been sitting in the same place, reading the paper and having breakfast, for approximately two hours.

"I know," she said, "but it just hit me that you are back. The guy I married is back."

I thought that was very nice. A moment. Maybe a milestone.

Two years into my civilian life, and by Kathy's measure, civility had been restored to my character. We all carry baggage and mine was certainly a busload after all those years. It was a remnant of the job for me, and for probably all of those with careers like mine. We all learn to deal with it in our own ways, or we don't.

My process for returning to civility was not a smooth one. My path was erratic and the beginning was particularly rough. There were some strange stops, and of course the strangest—and most unlikely—of all is the one that led to my second life in crime, as the *Homicide Hunter* (a name I've learned to live with) on the Investigation Discovery channel.

But that highly improbable adventure didn't begin until thirteen years after I left the Colorado Springs Police Department. My first stop was one that will likely surprise you as much as it surprised me.

I became a car salesman, maybe the least enthusiastic one in the history of the automotive industry. It was a brief but unproductive career. As I've noted, I did not go gently into retirement. I had a lot of built-up venom to drain. I trusted no one. My disposition ranged from unfriendly to surly. This did not serve me well in the first post-retirement job. I took it just a week or so after I left the department, which was probably too soon.

A good friend owned the car dealership. I always loved cars. I loved buying them, trading them, driving them, working on them. I've probably had more than fifty vehicles over the years. So I let my friend convince me to work for him. I promised to try it for a year.

Would you buy a car from a surly ex-homicide detective? Actually, I was pleasant to customers. I was more on their side than the dealerships, which didn't make me very popular in team meetings. I was also used to being the boss, and then I wasn't anymore. You can imagine how that went.

Exactly twelve months after taking the job, I stood up at a staff sales meeting and announced my resignation:

> "I won't be staying. I came from environment where doing the right thing was the only thing that mattered. Then I entered this environment, where making money is the only thing that matters. That's not to say you are evil, but if I continue to associate with you, then I would become like you. I am not like you and I don't want to be."

I wished them a pleasant afternoon and then I went home and did nothing for a couple of months except drive Kathy out of her mind.

Once again, she finally said either I get another job or she'd kill me.

"That would take a lot of paperwork," I said.

THE WALDORF-HYSTERIA

A few days later, she found jobs for both of us. She signed me up to be a part-time school bus driver. Kathy signed on as a "paraprofessional" monitor to assist school bus drivers in keeping peace and order on board.

I was assigned to the short bus with special needs kids. She was assigned to monitor what we referred to as "the convicts," older kids kicked out of regular school and shipped off to an alternative school.

I was the good-cop bus driver. She was the bad-cop monitor and driver's assistant. We loved these jobs. Mine proved to be great therapy. For the first time in my life, when I showed up at their doorsteps—and bus stops—people were glad to see me. That had rarely happened in my police career.

You might also be surprised to learn that I became a big fan of Disney tunes. We played them on my bus. We sang all the way to school, mostly songs from *The Little Mermaid* and *The Lion King*. I called it the Waldorf-Hysteria bus because everybody on it was crazy happy, including me.

It was the perfect job. I loved those little kids and they loved me back. It was very fulfilling. I didn't just pick them up and deliver them, I made a positive difference in their lives, or tried to.

I had one severely autistic kid, we'll call him Douglas, but that wasn't really his name. The only thing he wanted to talk to was the reflector on a fence post in his driveway. He spoke gibberish to it. But I taught him to do a high-five with me. I made contact with him. Something clicked. We practiced our high-fiving for a couple of days on the bus.

When I took Douglas home one day, his mother was waiting. I asked if her son and I could show her something. I said to him, "Gimme five, man!"

Douglas leaped up and slapped my hand. His mother cried.

Maybe I did, too, a little.

SMALL CRIMES AND MISDEMEANORS

Kathy and I didn't coddle our kids. We practiced tough love, but the emphasis was always on love, I think. Maybe I should let the kids answer that. At any rate, our bus-driving experiences opened our eyes to a wide range of parenting strategies. Some were extremely impressive and even inspiring. Others made you want to slap the parents and ask them what the hell they were thinking. The same was true with the way schools treated their kids.

I had a kid on my bus who had no medical issues, he wasn't disabled, he was just what they'd call an ADD kid, a little out of control, like most kids I grew up with. He was eight years old. They had him ride my bus as a way to keep him under control. They knew I ran a tight ship. One day when I was picking up kids, I saw that a teacher had him by the wrist. She had a grip on him.

He was glaring at me like I was the bad guy.

"Do you have his candy?" she asked.

Some of the kids were on medication, which they called "candy." So I wasn't sure what she was talking about. I told her I didn't have any prescription information for this one.

"No," the teacher said. "It's just candy, real candy."

"Why would I give him candy?" I asked.

I was just a dumb bus driver, after all.

"I told him if he behaves on the bus, you will give him candy," the teacher said.

"You told him that? Did you graduate from college?" I said.

I don't think Teacher expected Bus Driver to be so sassy. She gave me the death stare. It might have worked on grades one through five, but not on me.

"Come here, son," I said to the boy. "You can sit right next to me. There is no candy on this bus. If you behave and do what I tell you and act nice, I won't put knots on your head. Do you understand?"

"Yes," he said.

I told him that there might be people like the teacher who could be manipulated, but there were also people like me who knew that he was smart enough to follow the rules when he wanted to. I explained that it was in his best interest to control himself instead of having me control him.

He nodded in agreement.

"Okay, please go sit down."

From that day forward, he called me Mr. Joe. He sat down and behaved perfectly. We became buddies because I defined our roles. Him, kid. Me, bus driver. I didn't put up with any crap and he appreciated having his boundaries established.

Everyone was amazed. I'm sure scholarly papers were written on his miraculous recovery, without mentioning me, of course.

There was another kid who was a bit more of a hard case. He was older, about ready to age out from childhood into legal adulthood. He was standing outside my bus, preparing to board while smoking a cigarette.

"Put that out," I said.

"You gonna make me," he said.

"Are you bulletproof?" I responded.

"No!"

"Then you'd better put out the fucking cigarette."

He threw down the cigarette, stomped on it, and got on the bus with a full head of steam. I followed him, just in case he was planning on making trouble on my bus. He sat down with a sour face, glaring at me.

"Hey, kid," I said softly. "Prison wasn't so bad. I wouldn't mind going back if I had to."

His face went pale.

"Have you ever been in a fight for your life? Probably not, but if you get up out of your seat just once, you will find out what it's like and you won't enjoy it."

"Yes, sir," he said.

I never had to say another word to him. We had an understanding. I didn't take any crap. Except from Emmitt. There was just something about him. I think it was his aim. I really admired his aim.

He was six. He had problems, but this kid could hit any target as long as he was throwing his favorite missile, his tennis shoe. He'd sit in the back of bus, wing it at me, and knock my hat off every day.

Then he'd laugh and laugh.

So would I.

Emmitt never missed. I liked that.

I had another interesting kid, one of my older riders. He was fifteen or so. For the longest time, I couldn't figure out why he was on my bus. He was articulate and bright. The first day of school he said, "Mr. Joe, I understand you are my driver this year. I'm very pleased to be on this bus and I want you to be aware that kids on the bus have problems and I will be happy to assist you anyway I can."

I thanked him and he sat down. He sounded like a thirty-year-old lawyer. He was helpful. He kept the little ones in their seats. He talked to them and kept things to a low roar. I wondered what was going on with him. He didn't seem troubled at all.

Then one day I had to stop for a flagman in a construction zone. My young helper hustled up from his seat. For the first time, he seemed anxious.

"Are we going to be late for school?"

"Maybe a little," I said.

He returned to his seat, picked up a backpack, and threw it at me. Then he screamed like a banshee and threw more backpacks at the windshield. I went to him, wrapped my arms around him, hugged him, and told him it would be okay. When I felt him relax, I asked if I could let him go. He said yes, apologized, and returned quietly to his seat. I tried to never be late again, and he was fine.

Like a lot of us, he didn't like his routine disrupted.

I could identify with that.

RETURNING TO THE SCENES OF MY CRIMES

Driving the bus was a joy. Summers and holidays off. The pay was lousy and I didn't care. I had my retirement checks and the kids were out of the house and on their own. I felt like I was making a positive difference. Parents knew their children were safe with me.

For nine years, Kathy and I settled into a blissful routine of normalcy. We worked a little, played a little, and let go of painful memories as best we could. I didn't want to ever go back and stir up the darkest of my days as a cop, or so I thought.

Then Kathy made me respond to some pesky producer guy who had this crazy idea about doing a reality television show about a real-life homicide detective's experiences. I ignored the producer dude until my wife got mad at me.

Then we talked. Then I talked to his camera for a test run that went pretty well, and I've been talking to cameras ever since. I did hang on to my bus-driving job for a year, to make sure the new gig wasn't some sort of weird dream.

Maybe it is, but it's working for me. Talking about my life of crime is cathartic. It's brought me closer to peace than I've been in a long, long time.

My wife and kids say I'm a different man now. More fun to be around.

I'd have to agree that I am having more fun.

My career path wasn't one I'd recommend to anyone: from homicide detective to car salesman, to school bus driver to television star. But the way things have turned out, I'm really starting to believe that there is some justice in this old world.

A PARTING TALE

One more story before we say so long until next time.

Since I've shared so many nightmare tales with you, I thought it would be a good idea to give you something a little more upbeat as a parting gift. This is a story about a couple of very good days, maybe the best two days of my career as a cop in Colorado Springs.

They were twenty years apart, but hey, you take 'em when you can get 'em.

I was still a patrolman way back during one of the worst winters we experienced. A horrible blizzard rolled down from the Rockies and just buried the entire town and surrounding area. It snowed for three days. The wind came howling down like an avalanche. There were ten-foot drifts everywhere.

Even though we were accustomed to harsh winter weather and heavy snow, this massive storm paralyzed the entire region. The governor had declared the entire state a disaster zone.

All residents were advised to stay in their homes. Police, fire, and EMT personnel were dispatched only in extreme emergencies and had to use special equipment to get through the deep snow and terrible conditions.

Our particular piece of special equipment was a military-surplus M-60A1 "Patton" tank. Forty-nine tons of treads and turrets with a 750-horsepower engine and a top speed of 30 miles per hour. Did I mention the 104mm M68 cannon, backed up by a two machine guns?

Now that was my kind of snowplow!

The tank was provided by Fort Carson along with an active-duty crew to support our efforts during the storm. They'd just arrived when we were dispatched to assist a pregnant woman and transport her from a snowbound home to the hospital delivery room. I climbed aboard the tank, feeling like a real hero as I stood up in the turret.

The winds were too high for a helicopter. They couldn't get an ambulance through the snow. So we rolled into the storm and conquered it like General Patton liberating France from the Nazis.

It was a blast busting through drifts and waving to the citizens huddled in their homes. We heroically arrived at the doorstep of the pregnant woman and I heroically waded through the snow into the house. I then heroically carried the lady back to the tank where, unlike General Patton, I promptly lost the Battle of the Bulge.

The woman's substantial baby bump made it impossible for us to get her into the tank's hatch. We tried every which way to fit her through it—head first, feet first. There was just no way we could squeeze her and her whopping belly into the tank.

I felt somewhat less heroic carrying her back into the house. The baby didn't care about any of our shenanigans. He was coming whether we were ready or not. I changed hats from tank commander to amateur ob/gyn. I brought the bouncing baby boy into the snow-white world.

Mother and child survived my lack of medical training. Once they were no longer contained in one body, we managed to fit them both into the tank and hauled ass to the waiting arms of real doctors and medical staff.

It was a landmark day in my young career, one that was quickly buried in many much less memorable and darker days. And then another day came twenty years later. By then I was head of the major crimes division, where two secretaries guarded my door from walk-in crazies and the outraged mothers of bloodthirsty criminals.

"Lieutenant, there is a woman outside and she insists on seeing you."

"Tell her to go away or I'll shoot her between the eyes," I said.

"She doesn't seem hostile. She seems normal, and she has a young man with her who seems very nice."

"What do they want?"

"She won't say, but she seems pleasant enough."

"Let them in, but call me with an emergency in ten minutes, so I can get them out of here if need be."

I was expecting the worst, thinking this was probably some mother whose son we busted for pot or exposing himself to the girl's lacrosse team.

They walked in.

"Hi, Lieutenant Kenda, do you remember me?" said the mother.

"No, I'm afraid I don't," I said.

"Then I suppose you don't remember him, either," she said, nodding to the young man.

He looked like a nice kid. I shook his hand.

"Is he your son?"

"You should know," she said. "The last time you saw him, you'd just brought him into the world."

I closed the door after telling my secretaries to hold all my calls. She'd wanted me to meet her son, who was by then twenty years old, six foot, two inches tall, and bound for college.

She'd had other children since, and the day the policeman came in a tank and delivered the oldest child was part of family legend.

We talked for an hour or so and it was lovely, just lovely. There weren't many days when it felt good to be in that office. This was one of those rare occasions. Usually, it was someone telling me why they hated me.

This was different, and it was wonderful, a truly wonderful day that I will always savor.

ACKNOWLEDGMENTS

This book would not exist were it not for some very important people.

My wife, Kathy, always pleaded with me to write a book. Okay, the truth: She nagged me nonstop for thirty years. This is the result.

Jan and Austin Miller, who are literary agents in Dallas, Texas, believed I had something to say. You can be the judge of whether I said it well.

Kate Hartson, my editor at Hachette Book Group, read it with the practiced eye of a true professional. Her guidance and advice have been invaluable.

The true wizard in this effort is my ghostwriter, D. Wesley Smith. Over many months of nonstop interviews, Wes was able to capture my voice in words on the page. A rare and wonderful skill of a true wordsmith.

I also consider him my friend.

This book is in reality our book.

I hope you enjoyed reading it.

JOE KENDA is retired at the rank of lieutenant from the Colorado Springs Police Department. He conducted criminal investigations involving violent crime for more than twenty of his twenty-five years of service.

He served as a detective, detective sergeant, detective lieutenant, and finally commander of the Major Crimes Unit. Joe achieved a solution rate of 92 percent of the 387 homicide cases assigned to him and his unit. He is a certified instructor in the state of Colorado for Criminal Investigations, Advanced Criminal Investigations, Multi-Jurisdictional Investigations, Patrol Operations, and Specialized Patrol Operations. Kenda is a member of the executive board of the American Investigative Society of Cold Cases and actively participates in offering advice to agencies with cold cases involving murder.

Since 2011, he has starred in a television series on Investigation Discovery network. Titled *Homicide Hunter: Lt. Joe Kenda*, the show is currently filming twenty episodes for its sixth season. The first three seasons are currently being broadcast in more than 183 countries and in more than one hundred languages.

Joe is married with two adult children. He and his wife, Kathy, reside in the Tidewater area of Virginia.